Cultivating Values in Startup

Sybil G. Bahr

Abstract

The purpose of this study was to explore the artifacts, norms, values, and underlying assumptions within the organizational culture of a startup athletic apparel company. Utilizing Edgar Schein's organizational culture framework, a case study was performed to examine the processes, strategies, and values used by company founders and leaders to create and sustain an organizational culture. Podcast interviews were used to collect data from company founders and departmental leaders. Document analysis of website data allowed the researcher to examine company structures and processes. A survey of employees in non-leadership positions provided data organizational culture data from those participants within the organization. Survey responses yielded a 50% response rate with 40 participants. The podcasts provided data from two co-founders and 12 departmental leaders. Results found the theoretical framework from previous organizational culture research was evident in a startup company's culture framework. However, the case study revealed elements of organizational culture within the startup company utilized a horizontal flow between artifacts, norms, values, and assumptions versus a vertical, top-down flow of those elements. The organizational culture of the startup company centered around themes of transparency and communication with a consistent focus and application of each of the levels of the framework working as one. The focus on organizational culture from company founders and leaders was people focused. Results determined the people-focused approach was consistent with the survey responses from employees in non-leadership positions.

Keywords: organizational culture, startup company, values, leadership, creating organizational culture, sustainable organizational culture

Dedication

To Toby, Lasher, and Haven, for your support, encouragement, and grace while I pursued this degree. I could not have done this without your patience and the sacrifices you made to make this happen for me. I feel extremely lucky to have a husband and children as amazing as you.

To my parents, Richard and Jackie Lasher, who instilled in me the work ethic, the confidence, and the virtue of always finishing what you start, regardless of the challenge. Your support and love are unwavering, and I am forever thankful.

To my aunt, Peggy Lasher, your dedication to education was admirable. I wish you were here to celebrate with me.

Acknowledgements

I would like to express my sincere appreciation and gratitude to my dissertation committee, Dr. Robert Doan, Dr. Natalie Cruz, and Dr. Julie Fernandez. Your accessibility, candid feedback, and guidance throughout this process exceeded expectations. I am thankful to have had a committee of down-to-earth, realistic, and genuine people to guide me through this project.

I am grateful to the professors in the program and my fellow Cohort C members. Pursuit of this degree always felt like a team and a family working towards a common goal. I am thankful for your guidance, your friendship, and the lessons I learned from each one of you during this journey.

To friends and fellow students, Frank Monterisi and Delane Neuroth. Frank, you were the best class project partner and friend throughout the pursuit of this degree. I enjoyed working with you on every project. Your work ethic, sense of humor, and zest for life made class work fun. Delane, I appreciate your guidance, support, and friendship throughout this journey. This process would not have been the same without someone to laugh with.

Lastly, to my mom, Jackie Lasher. Thank you for showing me that a mother with children can go back to school and pursue a degree. You did it when I was a kid, and you were my inspiration for attempting this degree while raising a family. Thank you for being a role model.

Table of Contents

Abstract i

Copyright Page ii

Dedication iii

Acknowledgements iv

List of Tables ix

Lists of Figures x

Chapter One: Introduction 1

Overview 1

Background 2

Statement of the Problem 4

Statement of the Purpose 5

Significance of the Study 6

Research questions 8

Introduction to the Theoretical Framework 8

Definitions 10

Summary 11

Chapter Two: Review of the literature 14

Overview 14

Theoretical Framework 15

Foundations of Research on Organizational Culture 16

- Organizational Communication 19
- Organizational Growth Mindset 22
- Organizational Change 23
- Organizational Symbolism 25

Modern approaches to studies of organizational culture 28
- Organizational Health 28
- Daring Leadership 32
- Inspirational Leadership 34

The Influence and Impact of Leadership on Organizational Culture 37
- Leader Communication 44
- Personality of Organization, Leadership, and Employees 47

Followership and Building Teams 50
- Principles of Followership 51
- Building Teams 53
    - Values 57
    - Communication Methods within Organizations 59
    - Elements of a Startup 61

Summary 62

Chapter Three: Research Methodology 65

Overview 65

Design 65

Research Questions 66

Setting	66
Participants	69
Sampling	70
Procedures	71
The Researcher's Role	74
Instruments	76
Data Collection	78
Data Analysis	79
Trustworthiness	82
Credibility	82
Dependability and Conformability	82
Transferability	83
Triangulation	83
Ethical Considerations	84
Delimitations	84
Summary	85
Chapter Four: Findings	87
Overview	87
Research Questions	88
Results	89
Data Analysis and Themes	90
Organizational Structures and Processes	92

Company Values, Strategies, and Goals 98

Actions, Perceptions, and Beliefs Within the Company 102

Summary 114

Chapter Five: Discussion and Conclusion 117

Overview 117

Summary of Findings 117

Artifacts 119

Norms and Values 121

Underlying Assumptions 123

Discussion 126

Implications 128

Limitations 129

Recommendations for Future Research 130

Summary 133

List of Tables

Table 1: Organization of the Case Study Elements 89

Table 2: Podcast Interviews with Company Leaders...92

Table 3: Defined Values for Each Department..99

Table 4: Length of Employment at Startup Company...106

Table 5: Participant Age 107

Table 6: Participant Gender 107

Table 7: Level of Education..108

Table 8: Current Employment Status..108

Table 9: Employee Descriptions of Company Leaders: Positive and Negative
        Descriptions 110

Table 10: Employee Suggestions for Changes Related to Culture 113

Table 11: Open-Ended Survey Questions and Schein's Framework Element 114

List of Figures

Figure 1: Lencioni's Four Disciplines Model 31

Figure 2: Illustration of Schein's Model of Organizational Culture 41

Figure 3: Illustration of Schein's Model of Organizational Culture 90

Figure 5: A Comparison of Schein's Framework to Startup Company
Framework 116

Figure 6: A Comparison of Schein's Framework to Startup Company
Framework 126

Chapter One: Introduction

Overview

Organizational culture is a dynamic phenomenon being constantly enacted and created by interactions with others and shaped by leadership behavior. The set of structures, routines, rules, and norms that guide behavior are the catalysts for creating and sustaining organizational culture (Schein, 2004). The founder or entrepreneur will initiate visions, goals, beliefs, values, and assumptions of an organization from the beginning. The culture formation will revolve around that leader. Designing an organizational culture has infinite possibilities yet is always relevant. For a culture to be vibrant and sustainable, it must come from the blood, from the soul (Horowitz, 2019). As the shared experiences of the group or groups within the organization grow through behavioral, emotional, and cognitive elements, the functioning organizational culture will form from the founder or entrepreneur's efforts to guide and instill a culture within the organization (Schein, 2004).

Recent research by Wright (2019) on startup companies and organizational culture focused on leader behaviors, creation of organizational norms, and support of innovative mindsets for all employees. The author noted a story about Dean Smith, the legendary men's basketball coach at the University of North Carolina. Coach Smith recruited the most talented players for his basketball program. Upon the first meeting between Coach Smith and his players, there was a recurring pattern of players wearing their high school letter jackets. Despite their insight, efforts, goals, and success in high school basketball, Coach Smith required the players to send their high school jacket back home as a visible artifact of their transition to a new system and a new program, college basketball at the University of North Carolina (Wright, 2019). The author used the story to display a practice associated with the creation of norms, artifacts, and beliefs in a new organization.

The purpose of this case study was to explore how artifacts, norms and values, and underlying assumptions create and reinforce the organizational culture developed by the founder and leader of the company (Schein, 2004). The subject of this research study was a startup athletic apparel business based in Los Angeles, California. Data were collected from pre-recorded podcast interviews, document analysis, and surveys to determine values, behaviors, and communication practices within the startup company and the impact on the organizational culture within the company. Lundstrom and Lundstrom (2021) determined podcasts a phenomenon with a rampant cultural impact due to their intersection of the digital and non-digital worlds. The researcher utilized modern data collection methods to explore the elements of the organizational culture of the startup athletic apparel company.

Background

This study examined principles and practices of creating and sustaining organizational culture in a startup athletic apparel business. The impact of culture within an organization is a critical element in day-to-day business practices (Burkus, 2014). The values and assumptions shaping culture guide activities and group norms within the organization (Schein, 2004). Attributes of creating and sustaining a strong, positive culture are of value to leaders in a variety of settings. Cultures are aspirational, and total cultural compliance or harmony is unrealistic. The point is to not to be perfect, just be better than yesterday (Horowitz, 2019).

So goes the culture, so goes the company. (Sinek, 2017, p. 159). Culture has been a long-time focus of anthropologists as they seek to understand different groups. Only recently, organizational researchers have begun to discover the links between culture, the performance of organizations, and the behaviors, attitudes, and values of people in organizations (Warrick, 2017). Culture expresses goals through values and beliefs and guides activity through shared assumptions and group norms. Founders and influential leaders set culture in motion and imprint values and assumptions that persist for decades (Groysberg et al., 2018).

Culture has recently been recognized as a significant factor in the success of organizations. Surveys conducted to determine the best places to work in the United States are increasingly based on information employees anonymously report about their workplace culture (Warrick, 2017). Within a strong corporate culture, employees will form attachments by identifying with the company in a very personal way. Employees feel a sense of belonging. Sinek (2017) used an example of a t-shirt. A t-shirt stamped with the company logo could be used to sleep in or wear while painting the house. Or, if the employee has a sense of belonging, that person will wear the company logo in public with pride.

A strong culture describes a culture that has a significant influence on the behaviors and practices of employees (Warrick, 2017). In contrast, a weak culture is one in which the norms and practices are not well known or are confusing, inconsistent, and not reinforced. When founders and leaders focus on creating a strong culture, higher performance outcomes are often the result (Warrick, 2017). Founders and leaders fostering a weak culture find employees veer away from doing the right thing in favor of doing the thing that is right for them as an individual (Sinek, 2017).

A unique cultural analogy used to articulate standards within a culture can be exhibited by a glass of milk. Sinek (2017) determined when organizational culture standards shift from character, values, and beliefs to a specific focus only on performance, numbers, and other impersonal dopamine-driven measurements, behavior-focused chemicals fall out of balance, and one's will to trust and cooperate dilutes. The author attested those actions are like adding water to a glass of milk. Eventually, the culture becomes so watered down it loses all that makes it good and healthy. The result is a glass of liquid that only vaguely looks and tastes like milk.

The culture of a company defines its value to those who know it. Performance metrics can go up and down, but the strength of a culture is the only thing organizations can truly rely on (Sinek, 2017). Cultures are like precious and prized treasures when they are strong, healthy, and driving the right behaviors. They are among the greatest assets and organization can have (Warrick, 2017).

Statement of the Problem

When organizational cultures are strong, healthy the value for individual employees and the workplace team as a unit is a treasure. Cultures are vulnerable assets that can be damaged or lost if leaders and founders of organizations are not aware or attentive to the value of a strong culture (Warrick, 2017). Culture can overcome the seemingly invincible structural barriers of an era and transform the behavior of entire industries and social systems. Jeff Bezos created Amazon with the strategic element of a low-cost structure. The result was a culture attune to frugality. In contrast, Apple was created with a strategic vision of building the most beautiful, perfectly designed products in the world. A culture of frugality would have been counterproductive to Apple's vision and goals as a creator and provider of innovative products (Horowitz, 2019).

Understanding the elements of creating and sustaining a strong organizational culture are of value to companies, businesses, and teams within a variety of industries. The performance of a company is closely tied to the personality and values of the leader or founder. That personality and set of values sets the tone for the culture (Sinek, 2017). Leadership is about taking responsibility for lives and not numbers, a focus on people. From that focus, organizations can build strong cultures. The personality and values of the person at the top of the organizational chart sets the tone for culture (Sinek, 2014). The leadership determines what the organization does. What you do is who you are, your culture (Horowitz, 2019).

Statement of the Purpose

The purpose of this study was to explore how artifacts, norms and values, and underlying assumptions create and reinforce the organizational culture of a startup athletic apparel company based in California (Schein, 2004). By conducting a case study about this company, the researcher intended to examine the elements of organizational culture from the perspectives of founders, leaders, and employees to determine how each element impacts the creation and sustainability of the organization's culture. Culture can be built by design or by default. A lack of attentiveness to the elements of creating and fostering a positive, strong organizational culture result in the culture creating itself. To purposefully build a strong culture, the desired cultural values should be identified and made known. Education for group members on the cultural ideals coupled with communication and reinforcement, is the foundation of building a strong culture (Warrick, 2017). This study was designed for the researcher to explore the culture within a startup company to understand how the founders, leaders, and employees contribute to the overall organizational culture. Results from this study would be beneficial for organizations, companies, and teams in a variety of industries. Whether a company is a startup or a hundred years old, designing culture is always relevant (Horowitz, 2019).

Significance of the Study

Results from this study would be beneficial as a guide for teams, departments, and companies seeking knowledge and practical initiatives to create, change, and develop the organizational culture within their businesses. This research aimed to define processes and procedures dedicated to culture creation within a startup company that could be used by other organizations as a guide for intentionally focused organizational culture building. Company leaders are responsible for understanding the present culture within organizations to reinforce strengths and address weaknesses and inconsistencies. Evaluation of the culture within an organization is of great value and can be accomplished by observing and experiencing the culture to seek insights on strengths and weaknesses (Warrick, 2018). The significance of choosing the subject company for this study was the leader focus on the uniqueness of the company. Creating and sustaining an organizational culture comes with other people having ideas of what a company should be. If implementation of ideas is inconsistent with company beliefs and personality, organizational culture suffers (Horowitz, 2019). The result is an importance of leader attentiveness to, and study of organizational culture.

Schein (1983) determined an organizational culture depends for its existence on several people interacting with each other for the purpose of accomplishing some goal in their defined environment. The founder of the organization shapes the culture and guides the organization through crises of growth and survival resulting in development of organizational culture. Leaders inform and create culture through values, rituals, and rules they put into practice (Hocking, 2021). Organizations are differentiated by culture in that company culture can drive or diminish inclusivity, flexibility, trust, and innovation.

Attributes of culture creation assist leaders in building a foundation for training and development programs within the organization. A foundation of values and communication practices allows leaders and companies to be agile and relevant during challenging times. The significance of understanding the content of culture is to study the attributes and application of values, norms, and artifacts (Schein, 1990). Organizations are social fields where complex discourses of information and knowledge are produced and communicated. To gain understanding of organizations, it is necessary to analyze them from the outside versus what is already organized (Mills et al., 2001). Using a case study method to study organizational culture through open-ended interviews can get to the level of how people feel and think versus questionnaires and surveys with predetermined dimensions to be studied (Schein, 1990). Creating and sustaining an organizational culture is applicable to teams, companies, and businesses in a variety of professional settings. Whether a startup company, or an established business, this research could be utilized by many organizations to improve the creation and foundation of their culture.

Research Questions

This study examined how structures, processes, values, actions, and practices create and reinforce organizational culture within a startup athletic apparel organization. The subject of the study was a startup company based in Los Angeles with founders and leaders intentionally focus on the internal organizational culture. The research questions are:

RQ1: What are the organizational structures and processes that contribute to the creation and sustainability of the organizational culture?

RQ2: What are the values, strategies, and goals that determine the organizational culture at the startup athletic apparel company?

RQ3: What are actions, perceptions, and beliefs within the culture that are mutually reinforced by leaders and employees?

Introduction to the Theoretical Framework

The researcher conducted this case study by examining the artifacts, norms, values, and assumptions as defined by the leaders and employees of the startup athletic apparel company (Schein, 2004). The examination and exploration of the elements of organizational culture included data collection from all levels within the company. Company founders, departmental leaders, website data, and employees in non-leadership positions provided insight necessary to thoroughly examine the overall impact on the creation and sustainability of the organization's culture. Schein's (2004) model of organizational culture was the theoretical framework for this study. From decades of extensive research, three levels of culture are determined as the foundation of this model: artifacts, espoused values and beliefs, and underlying assumptions.

Schein (2004) defined artifacts as all the phenomena that one sees, hears, and feels when one encounters a new group with an unfamiliar culture. Artifacts are visible, organizational structures and processes. Espoused beliefs and values are strategies, goals, and philosophies. The researcher determined those elements required social validation by the group or organization members. As the group learned the beliefs and values initially instituted by the founders and leaders, those beliefs and values became norms. Schein's (2004) framework attested beliefs and values at the conscious level will predict much of the behavior that is observed at the artifacts level.

The third level of Schein's (2004) framework was underlying assumptions. Underlying assumptions are like theories-in-use. Assumptions are those elements and processes that are so strongly held in a group that members will find behavior based on any other premise inconceivable. Underlying assumptions make up the culture of a group and can be thought of at both the individual and group levels as psychological cognitive defense mechanisms that permit the group to continue to function. At this level, culture can be thought of as the organization's DNA (Schein, 2004).

Schein (1990) attested organizational culture is a force. Groups and organizations do not form accidentally or spontaneously (Schein, 1983). When culture is a priority for founders and leaders of organizations, the phenomenon can greatly impact the members of the organization. Horowitz (2019) noted whether a company is a startup or well-established, designing culture is always relevant. When leaders focus on culture as a relevant effort, organizations evolve to meet new challenges.

This study examined how structures, processes, actions, goals, and strategies of a startup company attribute to the creation and sustainability of assumptions, values, and artifacts of the Schein (1990) model of organizational culture. The researcher gained this knowledge through data obtained from podcast interviews conducted by the founders of the startup and departmental leaders. In addition, document analysis was performed to allow the researcher to further examine and explore values, areas of focus, and communication practices within the startup organization as presented on the official company website. Lastly, surveys were administered to company employees in non-leadership positions to complete a full review of the culture of the subject startup company.

Definitions

Artifacts–the overt and obvious elements of an organization. The things an outsider can see such as furniture and office layout, dress norms, and mantras (Burkus, 2014).

Culture–a pattern of shared basic assumptions that was learned by a group as it solved its problems of external adaptation and internal integration. The pattern has worked well enough to be considered valid and, therefore, to be taught to new members as the correct way to perceive, think, and feel in relation to those problems (Schein, 2004).

Followership–fundamental roles that individuals shift into and out of under various conditions. Leadership and followership are closely intertwined. Organizational success is achieved by having people who willingly and effectively follow just as people must willingly and effectively lead (Daft, 2018).

Influence–the relationship among people is not passive, but multidirectional and noncoercive (Daft, 2018).

Leadership–an influence relationship among leaders and followers who intend real changes and outcomes that reflect their shared purposes (Daft, 2018).

Norms–a frame of reference for what is acceptable and not acceptable within an organization. An informal standard of conduct that is shared by team members and guides their behaviors (Daft, 2018).

Startup–rooted in innovation, a startup aims to create a new template, product, or service. Distinguished by speed and growth, startup companies build ideas quickly and continuously change and improve based upon feedback and data (Baldridge & Curry, 2022).

Teams–a unit of two or more people who interact and coordinate their work to accomplish a shared goal or purpose to which they are committed and hold themselves mutually accountable (Daft, 2018).

Underlying assumptions–the beliefs and behaviors so deeply embedded that they can often go unnoticed. The essence of culture (Burkus, 2014). Assumptions are taken-for-granted, underlying, and usually unconscious. They determine perceptions, thought processes, feelings, and behaviors within organizations (Schein, 1990).

Values–fundamental beliefs that an organization or individual considers to be important. Values are stable over time and have an impact on attitudes, perception, and behavior (Daft, 2018).

Summary

Intentional, honest, strategic insights into organizational culture provide employees and prospective employees a level of purpose in their work and a positive well-being (Hocking, 2021). This research aimed to provide insight on intentional and strategic measures of culture in a startup company. The existence of an organizational culture depends on several people interacting with each other for the purpose of accomplishing some goal in their defined environment (Schein, 1983). Understanding and implementing the virtues of a business or company is the responsibility of the leaders. Leaders focused on action-based virtues versus belief-based virtues provide a solid foundation for companies and employees to contribute to building a sound organizational culture (Horowitz, 2019).

    Utilizing a case study method to study organizational culture through open-ended interviews reaches the level of how people feel and think versus questionnaires and surveys with predetermined dimensions to be studied (Schein, 1990). Culture could be uncovered with questions about company agility and adaptation to change, team connectiveness in remote or hybrid work settings, employee recognition, promotion of or sharing of failures, presence of difficult conversations, and incorporation of diversity and inclusion actions (Hocking, 2021). Creating and sustaining an organizational culture is applicable to teams, companies, and businesses in a variety of professional settings. This research could be utilized by many organizations of all sizes to improve the foundations of their culture.

    Chapter Two reviews historical and current research on organizational culture. The chapter provides a focus on the connections between Schein's (1983) framework on organizational culture and modern research encompassing leadership and the impact of leaders on organizational culture. The literature review is written as a guide for the reader to understand the progression of organizational culture research as it has adapted to societal changes throughout history.

Chapter Three details modern technology, podcasts, as a data collection medium for this research study. The researcher will detail use of podcasts, document analysis, and a survey to triangulate data for this case study on a startup athletic apparel company. Each data collection instrument will be attributed to collecting information from employees within different levels of the company organizational structure with the perspective of Schein's (2004) organizational culture framework.

Chapter Four provides a summary of findings from each data collection method. Each method provides insight on the subject company's culture from the perspective of various levels of employees. Utilizing tables and figures to synthesize data coupled with quotes from participants provides the reader with a comprehensive analysis of the subject company's organizational culture methods, processes, and strategies.

Chapter Five outlines the findings to include discussion, implications, and recommendations for future research. Case study findings combined with insight on societal impacts of the timing of this study provide the reader an understanding of the profound impact of attentiveness to organizational culture within all levels of a company. The relevance of the impact of this study is discussed along with the necessity for leaders to always strive to make impactful decisions to improve processes and strategies related to culture.

Chapter Two: Literature Review

Overview

The creation and sustainability of an organization's culture is a shared group phenomenon. Culture does not exist within a single person or within individual characteristics. It resides in shared behaviors, values, and assumptions experienced through norms and expectations of a group (Groysberg et al., 2018). Organizational culture is pervasive, enduring, and implicit. The creation and manifestation of a culture is influenced by collective behaviors, physical environments, visible symbols, and stories. The unseen aspects of culture development include mindsets, motivations, and unspoken assumptions (Groysberg et al., 2018).

Research dedicated to examining organizational cultures includes traditional focus on values, mission, and goals (Greer & Shuck, 2020). In addition, researchers examine organizational health by assessing agility and ability to change, emotional intelligence, personality types, and implementation of principles impacting values of every person within the organization. Dimensions applicable to the study of organizational culture regardless of type, size, industry, or geography are people interactions and response to change. From those dimensions, culture research aims to identify characteristics that determine the framework of creation and sustainability of culture. Characteristics such as caring, purpose, learning, enjoyment, results, authority, safety, and order are powerful in defining values of the company, the leaders, and the employees (Groysberg et al., 2018). Researchers studying organizational culture should understand societal beliefs and practices that work their way into organizations and impact culture (Wang & Loundsbury, 2021). The literature review accounted for societal shifts and guides the reader from early organizational culture research of Schein (1983) to more modern approaches to culture research from Brown (2018), Lencioni (2012), and Sinek (2009, 2014).

Theoretical Framework

Culture is a dynamic phenomenon being constantly enacted and created by interactions among employees and shaped by leadership behavior. Organizational culture is foundationally a set a structures, routines, rules, and norms that guide and constrain behaviors within companies, teams, and organizations (Schein, 2004). The theoretical framework for this study was Schein's (2004) model with three specific levels of culture. The first level, artifacts, are visible organizational structures and processes including formal descriptions of how the organization works, organization charts, and office layout. The author suggests this level of culture is both easy to observe, yet difficult to decipher. Artifacts within a culture can also include the dress code, the manner in which people address one another, the emotional intensity, company records, statements of philosophy, and annual reports (Schein, 1990).

The second level of Schein's (2004) model encompasses strategies, goals, and philosophies, deemed beliefs and values within the framework of culture. Within an organization's culture, if beliefs and values are congruent, the result can help bring the group together and serve as a source of identity and mission. The author attests beliefs, norms, and values typically involve the group's internal relations. The test of whether values and beliefs are working within an organization is determined by understanding how comfortable members of organization are when abiding by them.

The third level of Schein's (2004) framework is underlying assumptions. Assumptions are defined by the author as those taken-for-granted beliefs, perceptions, thoughts, and feelings of members of the organization, team, or group. Culture as a set of assumptions defines what to pay attention to, what things mean, how to react emotionally to what is going on, and what actions to take in various kinds of situations within an organization (Schein, 1990). The power of culture manifests in shared assumptions that are mutually enforced (Schein, 2004).

Schein's (2004) theoretical framework and extensive research on organizational culture demonstrates elements of studying an organization's culture. The author attested any group's culture can be studied at the three levels: artifacts, norms and values, and underlying assumptions. To decipher what is going on within an organization, there must be an understanding the meanings of each element of the framework, how the organization defines and lives each element, and which dimension is the most pertinent to the history of the organization (Schein, 1990).

Foundations of Research on Organizational Culture

An introductory basis for understanding organizational cultures is *The Golden Rule* as defined by Greer and Shuck (2020). The authors define the *Rule* as a way to challenge leaders to notice others, respond with dignity, be present in the moment, and live into real joy for the successes of others. Leaders modeling these practices showcase the importance of *The Golden Rule's* values and actions. Leaders' actions significantly impact the present and future culture within the organization.

Early culture research conducted by Bass and Avolio (1993), determined the importance of organizational culture was evident in every business unit because there is a constant interplay between culture and leadership. Everyday actions of leaders and subordinates dictate the culture as a force of growth and strength for an organization or a force of negative actions impacting abilities to be successful at all levels. Leaders create the mechanisms for cultural development by reinforcing norms and behaviors that determine boundaries of the organizational culture. A strong culture with distinct values allows for more autonomy at all levels and prevents top administrators from increasing personal power at the expense of others. There is a level of overall accountability, belonging, and cohesiveness in organizations with strong, positive cultures (Bass & Avolio, 1993).

Bennis (1989) determined change was the enemy for previous generations of business. Leaders attempted to prevent change as stability and consistency were paramount. Over the course of time, leaders understood change was inevitable and a sign of progress. The result was leader attention dedicated to embracing technology, global interdependence, mergers and acquisitions, demographics, and values. Human capital, people as a resource, was at the center of those challenging elements of change. The change in the perspective of leaders impacted business in the form of culture. Culture is the product of people and the infinite interactions that result when a group of people are brought together (Bryant, 2011).

Historical research about management was conducted by Peters (1987) prior to the term leadership becoming the norm. The author found managers served as a basis for leaders creating and building a positive, sustainable organizational culture. Guidelines were developed for managers and organizations to utilize during changing and challenging times in the business world. In addition, research provided suggestions for embracing change within an organization to include defining the organization's mission to frame its activities and inform its work force and create a flexible environment in which people are valued and encouraged to develop to their full potential. People should be treated as equals rather than subordinates. With a focus on long-term goals instead of short-term profit, leaders shape corporate culture, so creativity, autonomy, and continuous learning replace conformity. Leaders should constantly study the organization from the outside as well as the inside and encourage innovation, experimentation, and risk-taking. Lastly, Peters (1987) attributes proactive leadership versus reactive leadership as a means for success. Proactive approaches combined with global thinking and attentiveness to changing needs of the workforce all benefit the creation and sustainability of culture.

Schein (1986) determined culture was a deep phenomenon manifested in a variety of behaviors. The research of the author was focused less on traditional managerial styles and leadership types and more on his definitions of what constitutes organizational culture. Culture was defined as a pattern of basic assumptions that a group or organization has invented, discovered, or developed in learning to cope with its problems of external adaptation and internal integration. The organization determined those basic assumptions as valid, and they are taught to new members as the correct way to perceive, think, and feel in relation to organization issues and problem-solving methods (Schein, 1986). Efforts to determine, define, and implement actions related to organizational culture were significant in the foundation of organizational culture research by this author. The research established an early presentation of a how-to guide for organizations related to creating and sustaining organizational culture.

A practical application of foundational organizational culture research, a case study conducted by Auernhammer and Hall (2014) on a world-leading German automotive manufacturer, the authors determined organizational culture was influenced most significantly by three concepts: leadership style; behaviors centered around openness, motivation, and values; and behaviors within the organization related to mistakes and problems. Each of those concepts is related to critical events in the life and learning of the employees and leaders (Groysberg et al., 2018). The outcome observed in this study was specific to creativity and innovation. In the auto industry, and many of today's industries, a focus on place and freedom to create are considered aspects of a thriving culture (Auernhammer & Hall, 2014). In this case study, the implications of the findings are where strategy meets culture. The employees need to be supported by leadership to engage in the routine of their expertise and experience and periodically step out of the order and explore new ideas.

Organizational Communication

Leaders of organizations must understand communicating truthfully, confidently, and authentically connects them with their employees much like the rebar that supports the pillars of a bridge. In the case of an organization, communication is how the company proceeds from one side of a bridge to the other. Communication drives progress (Bustin, 2014). Leaders have acknowledged the need for relentless communication. Without it, employees have a way of filling in the blanks themselves and making incorrect assumptions (Bryant, 2011). Purpose and vision statements clearly and consistently communicated inspire confidence, forge solidarity, and serves as a catalyst for performance. Beyond those attributes of communication within an organization, clarity about every aspect of the organization forms what the leader believes and reinforces the role of each employee. The result is a unified workforce where everyone feels like part of team (Bustin, 2014). Communication is not merely a tool for leadership but leadership itself. Bryant (2011) stated it is an act of sharing information to create a sense of mission within the organization.

In a study of culture analytics published in the *Harvard Business Review*, researchers determined employee surveys and questionnaires about organizational cultures had significant shortcomings (Corritore et al., 2020). The researchers determined a new method for assessing organizational culture was to focus on communication within the organization. In one study, the researchers partnered with a midsize technology company to examine cultural fit between employees by reviewing linguistic styles in internal email messages. In another study conducted by Corritore et al. (2020), an analysis of Slack messages exchanged among members of software development teams provided insight on the impact of communication on culture. From a communication perspective, researchers reviewed email messages, Slack message exchanges and examined details categorized as diversity of thoughts, ideas, and meaning expressed by team members. Then, the researchers determined the impact, beneficial or detrimental, on the overall organizational culture of the company.

Organizational communication styles lead to cultural fit, cultural adaptability, and an understanding of values, norms, and behaviors integral to the operation of a company or organization. Understanding, evaluating, and focusing on communication as a culture analysis tool provides great potential for leaders to solve practical challenges inside organizations. Sharing understandings helps employees successfully coordinate with one another. From onboarding to everyday interactions, personally and electronically, leaders can reinforce communication standards and methods to impact organizational culture (Corritore et al., 2020).

A study conducted at a technical education institute by Gochhayat et al. (2017) examined the effect of organizational communication on organizational effectiveness and impacts of those variables on culture. Researchers determined a strong culture paves the way for improved communication, and better communication enhances organizational effectiveness. In the study, better communication was defined as establishment of a clear set of values and regulations for all stakeholders of the organization. Free flow of information on organizational values, beliefs, practices, and goals enhanced the environment within the organization. The subject organization in the study encouraged interactions, open discussions, and arguments as methods of obtaining consensus amongst employees, which minimized differences and further promoted open communication within the organization. In another study conducted by Gochhayat et al. (2017) within a technical education institute setting provided students, teachers, and support staff the knowledge, structure, and positive work environment to foster organizational effectiveness and open communication through a foundation of culture.

The value of organizational communication is deemed essential by organizational culture researcher Schein (1993). Modern studies of communication as those conducted by Corritore et al. (2020) focus on electronic communication amongst members of an organization. Schein (1993) conducted research on communication and deemed such research, a focus on dialogue. Dialogue was defined as a basic process for building common understanding to see the hidden meaning of words, first by seeing hidden meanings in our own communication as leaders. Researchers from Schein (1993) and Corritore et al. (2020) have determined the importance of communication, electronically and verbally, as a significant proponent of creating and sustaining organizational culture.

Organizational Growth Mindset

An organizational growth mindset is another perspective of research on organizational culture. In an article focused on the research of social psychologist Carol Dweck, the authors determined a growth mindset in the medical education field was necessary for an organizational culture framework for faculty and students that were the future of the medical workforce (Osman & Hirsh, 2021). Medical education is structural in a fixed performance mindset with regulations and rules determining actions. The authors note scientific revolutions arise when observations challenge accepted theories and norms are questioned and reimagined. Organizational culture within medical education institutions is profoundly impacted when learning and improvement includes taking risks, receiving feedback, and making corrections. Osman and Hirsh (2021) attested goals of progress and leadership must impact organizational culture through a growth mindset.

Defining culture with a growth mindset within an organization can be displayed in hiring practices. Horowitz (2019) noted a chief executive officer of a technology company looked for four attributes related to a growth mindset in potential employees. Interviews were set up to determine if prospective employees were smart people. Intelligence quotient was not measured. The person that was disposed toward learning was the right choice for the company. A second attribute the leader looked for was a humble person. People want you to succeed if you are humble. The foundation of humility creates the potential for individual and organizational growth. The last two attributes noted by the author for a growth mindset were hardworking and collaborative. Employees that work hard display the effort to be determined, resilient, and disciplined in their work. Those employees that are collaborative provide leadership throughout the ranks and encourage growth throughout the organization.

Schein (2006) authored an article detailing his 50 years of work and research on organizational culture. From the vast perspective of a comprehensive career of culture research, the author determined the growth of technology and globalization have produced more organizational dilemmas that require an agility within organizations to implement a growth mindset. Leaders of organizations will continue to endure the never-ending dilemma of individual versus the group, organization or society, and the understanding of whether leaders create organizations and cultures or whether culture and social forces create leaders. How organizations influence their members and how members change organizations must be approached from a growth mindset between the system and the individual (Schein, 2006). Lastly, Baldridge and Curry (2022) noted startups are characterized by rapid growth and a growth mindset.

Organizational Change

Organizational change and implementation of new practices has been researched related to organizational culture. Almeida et al. (2017) conducted a study in the construction industry in Brazil. The authors researched use of new technology, resistance to new technology, and the impact of culture on willingness of leaders and employees to embrace or resist change. The study determined there was a lack of interest in adopting new technology due to resistance to change by teams and a lack of planning and time. It was further concluded that internal factors of the organization hindered advancement because money-saving strategies were the focus versus a focus on innovation. The researchers noted organizational culture needed to be influenced by leadership through informing employees of the advantages and improvements they would acquire because of the changing technology.

Organizational change resides at the heart of leadership. Conceptual and process models of organizational change have been modified to reflect the role of cultural dynamics in leaders' efforts to influence the attitudes, norms, and behaviors of followers in organizational settings. Change impacts culture and can be utilized as a positive influence within an organization when the company is ready for change, creates a vision for change, develops implementation strategies, and assesses the impact of change for the organization and its culture (Latta, 2009).

In a study of complex social systems, Owen and Dietz (2012), determined the major reason for failure of organizations lies in the way decision makers think about and execute the change process. Change impacts and influences culture and vice versa because of the new patterns of relationships among members, new ways of behaving, and new processes for organizations and its members. The authors determined the importance of a focus on organizational change as a human process related to culture creation and sustainability requires leaders to look beyond rules and processes and focus on the human factor. Further, if leaders are not building a culture from the start of a company, one must know how to execute change to shift the culture via processes and the more important human factor.

Organizational Symbolism

Symbols are considered a reflection of an organization's culture because they provide clues about an organization's character, ideology, and value system (Cosar et al., 2020). In a study of a family-owned businesses in Turkey, Cosar et al. (2020) determined organizational symbolism of administrative and structural processes directly and positively affected organizational commitment and organizational performance. Outward symbols also directly and positively affected commitment and performance. The researchers defined outward symbols as the adaptation of the organization to environmental conditions, the ability to observe the environment and make decisions, relationships with customers, competition level with other businesses, the level of importance of social responsibility projects, reputation and image related to ethical codes, technology, and logos. The study determined organizational commitment was the bond created between the employees and the organization defined by loyalty and participation. The general results of the researchers' study on family-owned businesses determined the importance of organizational symbolism in hidden, implicit, and complex structures of culture. Symbols should be well interpreted by leaders and transferred in a positive way to have an integrative impact on the members of the organization.

A study conducted by Asatiani et al. (2018) on a small start-up company determined organizational culture was developed by symbolic and pragmatic action by the first employees and the founders of the company. As a small start-up, all employees were involved in all tasks. As the company experienced growth, it transformed into a globally distributed virtual organization. The leaders recognized their efforts to develop and maintain a positive organizational culture was being challenged by geographic distance and virtual work environments. The company leaders developed a culture code using taglines to provide symbolism to values. Through a series of exercises in interventions, feedback, and redevelopment, the company developed a handbook with experience-based narratives.

The Asatiani et al. (2018) study was conducted over the course of years to determine the impact of the digital organizational culture handbook used by the company being studied. The company used the handbook from the recruiting process and throughout the life of the organization, from start-up through growth, in the form of employee-management interactions and as a facilitator of discussions amongst employees. Recent updates and employee involvement in continued development of the handbook proved to be an impactful resource on the overall organizational culture in a virtual working environment. Similarly, in a study by Canning et al. (2020), the research determined employees were more satisfied with their organization's culture when it was determined the organization had a growth mindset versus a fixed mindset. In both studies, whether in-person or virtual, efforts to grow as an organization had implications on the organization's culture as perceived by the employees.

The studies by Cosar et al. (2020) and Asatiani et al. (2018) highlight the role of leaders and managers to interpret symbols in the organization and transmit them to organizational members in the correct way. Changing environmental factors led to a change in symbols as some disappear and new symbols emerge. Leaders of family-owned businesses to large corporations must focus on a constant renewal and update of focus on organizational symbols as people and processes change within organizations (Cosar et al., 2020).

The foundations of research related to organizational culture encompass a list of actions to be taken related to improving culture around the humans that make the organization operate to its maximum effectiveness. Optimal performance by a team or organization is related to its history, strategy, resources, and competitiveness. More importantly, assessment of culture is directly related to values, beliefs, and behaviors of its members. Assessment of culture across a range of individuals in different roles and levels is essential to understanding the impact of organizational culture on teams, programs, units, and organizations (Cruickshank & Collins, 2012).

Elements of creating and improving organizational culture have been evident for decades. The research by Peter (1987) was further examined by Bennis (1989) to determine an organization should function organically. Organizational purpose should determine its structure. Organizations should function as a community rather than a hierarchy, offer autonomy to its employees or members, provide opportunities and rewards, and understand the organization itself is the means, not the end. All elements of culture create one true mission for organizations of all types (Bennis, 1989). The intersection of leadership and culture is important as leaders chart the course for organizational culture. Schein's (1990) model of organizational culture encompasses the aspects of what a group learns over a period, including behaviors, symbols, and communication, as a determinant of problem solving related to the internal and external growth mindset as a catalyst for creating and sustaining the culture.

Modern Approaches to Studies of Organizational Culture

Modern research on the intersection of leadership and organizational culture has been studied by many in various contexts. Sinek (2009) determined leader actions and principles determine the "why" for employees inspiring actions towards organizational success. Lencioni (2012) researched the topic of organizational health to determine the impact of leaders on culture, or overall health, of a company. Brown (2018) conducted leadership research with a focus on the leader as a person beyond his or her duties to manage daily strategies and processes. The principles and findings on these topics by early researchers are evident in modern applications of understanding, creating, and sustaining organizational culture. The wealth of research indicates more leaders and organizations are open to assessment of their cultures with a focus on improvement for the humans within the organizations.

Organizational Health

Lencioni (2012) conducted research on leaders and organizations to determine the organizational health of businesses and team units within a business. A healthy organization was defined as one with minimal politics, minimal confusion, high morale, high productivity, and low turnover. The author's research led him to make a case for the value of organizational health with the statement, "The single greatest advantage any company can achieve is organizational health. Yet it is ignored by most leaders even though it is simple, free, and available to anyone who wants it." (Lencioni, 2012, p. 1). The health of an organization makes a difference in the lives of the employees and the impact on human capital will a competitive advantage and improved bottom line for the company.

Lencioni's (2012) research led to the development of four disciplines that must be maintained on an ongoing basis to preserve organizational health. The four disciplines include building a cohesive leadership team, create clarity, overcommunicate clarity, and reinforce clarity. The first discipline of building a cohesive team requires the leadership team to be behaviorally unified. From a large corporation to the department level, to small companies, churches, and schools, cohesion at the leadership level is essential to prevent dysfunction within the organization. The author used the analogy of family to demonstrate the need for cohesive leadership. If parents have a dysfunctional relationship as the leaders of the family unit, the family will not be able to realize its full potential.

The second discipline is to create clarity. Lencioni (2021) noted need for leaders of the organization to align levels of commitment and intellectual levels to provide a foundation for communication and understanding amongst the leaders. Without clarity, individuals do not work with one another, but on his or her own sets of assumptions on how to reach a goal or complete a task. Healthy organizations create so much clarity there is little room for confusion, disorder, and infighting. This discipline requires leaders to be clear about why they exist, how they behave, what they do, what determines success, important issues of the present, and accountability for specific job duties. Organizational health and culture measures and outcomes must be specific beyond words in a mission statement used for marketing purposes. The author concludes that healthy organizations have a team of leaders that understand more important than getting the right answer is to have an answer that they, employees, and the organization can commit.

Lencioni's (2012) third discipline is a building block of the second one. The need to overcommunicate clarity. Once the leaders create clarity amongst themselves, they must be able to communicate to employees and do so clearly, with enthusiasm, and repeatedly. The author determined through research that employees won't believe what leaders communicate to them until they have heard it seven times. There is never enough communication and overcommunication does not exist. A practical viewpoint by the author is provided in the determination great leaders see themselves as chief reminding officers as much as anything else. People embrace messages and information when they hear it over a period, in a variety of situations, and from different people. Overcommunicating clarity does include emails and presentations. The author attests cascading communication from leaders to the next level of managers, and throughout the organizational structure levels of the company must be consist, timely, and aligned.

The last element of Lencioni's (2012) model, reinforce clarity, is centered around the organization's values. Leaders should develop every policy, program, and activity to remind employees what is most important within the organization's operations. The researcher determined this must be done in every human system in the organization to insure positive culture and health of the company. Human systems include all processes from hiring to people management, training, and compensation. The author attributed human systems as the foundation that gives an organization structure for operations, culture, and management even when leaders are not present to remind and create clarity. The author's research determined behavioral values in a healthy organization must be aligned with hiring practices. Leaders with a focus on organizational health reinforce clarity by precisely knowing their values and using those values to hire the right people for their organization. The author included hiring process, orientation sessions, performance management systems, compensation systems, recognition, and rewards are elements of reinforcing clarity in the development of healthy organizations. Figure 1. is the Lencioni (2012) Four Disciplines Model from *The Advantage: Why Organizational Health Trumps Everything Else in Business:*

Figure 1

Lencioni (2012) Four Disciplines Model

Note. From *The Advantage: Why Organizational Health Trumps Everything Else in Business* (Lencioni, 2012).

Lencioni's (2012) research, reasoning, and clarification of impactful elements for creating and sustaining a healthy organization are of value to businesses of all sizes and settings. A level of commitment from all employees is required to function as a team with a focus on organizational health. The author concluded the single biggest factor determining whether an organization could improve its health is directly related to the commitment and active involvement of the person or people in charge. Organizational health within high-performing organizations requires principles of accountability from leaders followed by acting on those principles with consistency and urgency (Bustin, 2014).

Daring Leadership

Brown (2018) has done significant research on leaders, leadership, and organizational culture. One research study conducted on senior leaders began with a qualitative inquiry with the question, "What, if anything, about the way people are leading today needs to change in order for leaders to be successful in a complex, rapidly changing environment where we are faced with seemingly intractable challenges and an insatiable demand for innovation?" (Brown, 2018, p. 6).

One common response was most consistent across interviews from the researcher's study: the need for braver leaders and more courageous cultures. The researcher found the leaders discussed the concept of courage as a trait, not a behavior or skill. The subjects could not identify specific skills to build trust and courage, but could identify with passion, problematic behaviors, and cultural norms that corrode trust and courage. The author used the research to identify behaviors and cultural issues leaders attest get in the way of organizations across the world. Then, compared what the research team concluded was armored leadership actions versus daring leadership actions. An example of armored leadership is driving perfectionism and fostering fear of failure. In contrast, Brown (2012, p. 76-77) determined daring leadership as modeling and encouraging healthy striving, empathy, and self-compassion.

Understanding of the conclusions of armored leadership actions and daring leadership actions, mistakes were the catalyst for comparison of effective and ineffective leadership models (Brown, 2012). Research determined leaders avoid tough conversations including challenges with giving honest, productive feedback. Efforts to dimmish fears during times of stress were mistakenly reactive measures instead of proactive measures by leaders to control and maintain safety. Levels of trust between employees and leaders often eroded due to lack of connection and empathy from the leader. The risk of being ridiculed coupled with the risk of failure deterred employees from taking risks. The result for the organization was a lack of innovation and a creative mindset from employees at all levels of the organization.

Additional challenges determined by Brown's (2012) research found leaders spent too much time focusing on failures instead of moving on from setbacks. Levels of accountability for all employees coupled with learning opportunities prevented a culture of blame to permeate the company. The important aspect of diversity and inclusivity were being avoided due to fear of looking wrong, saying wrong, or being wrong. Leaders indicated problem-solving efforts were ineffective and unsustainable resulting in a costly ramification to employees and the culture. The realization that actual behaviors impacting the organization can be taught, measured, and evaluated versus focusing on values that are aspirations, not actions. Lastly, learning and growing for the good of the employees and culture was being hindered by perfectionism and fear. Each of the impacts of leader behavior or lack of action created a challenge for creating a sustaining a positive culture.

Bryant's (2011) research consisted of conversations and interviews with leaders of organizations. The researcher found the concept of being a coach, not a critic was impactful on organizational culture. As a coach, one must elevate individual players to make the team better. This is instituted by giving guidance and input on the front end, versus criticizing once employees make mistakes. Coaches provided feedback that was not personal, and this method resulted in employees knowing their leader had their best interests at heart and was on their side.

Brown (2012) further researched the leadership lessons to determine culture-building skill sets that could bring change to companies with deficient organizational cultures. The author described the list of issues as work behaviors and organizational concerns, but they were deeply human issues. The researcher and the research team developed instruments from their data to test action-based skills sets to improve organizational culture. Brown (2012) determined three skills leaders can build or attain to improve organizations. First, leaders must be vulnerable and willing to have conversations with an open mind and open heart, without egos. Second, leaders must be able to attain a level of self-awareness as a leadership behavior, not a trait or job title. Third, leaders must be courageous with a willingness to have tough conversations with open communication.

Brown (2012) developed, researched, and retested elements of leadership and issues and actions related to culture. This research is significant in modern leadership practices centered around organizational culture because it was tested on companies including the Gates Foundation, Shell, Fortune 50 companies, small family-owned businesses, and multiple branches of the United States Military. In summary, people report to managers, but they follow leaders (Bryant, 2011). To achieve extraordinary results, finding a place where personal values intersect with experience, interests, and company values can be the key to extraordinary results (Bustin, 2014).

Inspirational Leadership

In Sinek's (2009) book, *Start with why: How great leaders inspire everyone to take action,* revealed the personal calling to write a book about building organizational culture. The author's research on culture began with recognizing a pattern, way of thinking, acting, and communicating that gives leaders the ability to inspire others around them. A practical scenario the author used to demonstrate inspiration was a story about a group of American automobile executives. The car executives when to Japan to observe a Japanese assembly line. The end of the Japanese auto assembly line included putting the doors on hinges the same way the American assembly line operated. However, in the United States, an employee used a rubber mallet to tap the edges of the door to ensure a perfect fit. The American automobile executives noticed the difference between the steps in their assembly line and the Japanese assembly line. They inquired and the Japanese informed them they made sure the door fit when they designed it and did not need someone to tap it into place at the end of the assembly line. Sinek (2009) summarized this story noting the Japanese auto makers engineered the outcome they wanted from the beginning. They ensured the pieces fit from the start. The author builds the foundation for his research on the ideas that those that achieve more, influence more, build products, and create companies have a clear focus on recruiting people and executing processes based on original intentions. Leaders understanding that was stands in the way becomes way is a focus of implementing inspirational practices to impact culture (Brown, 2018).

The premise of leaders identifying "why" starts with a positive focus. Sinek (2009) determined efforts to improve leaders and organizational cultures should not start with fixing what is broken, but to determine what works and amplify those strengths within the organization. Research conducted by this author to understand the beginnings of successful people and successful companies allows today's leaders and organizations to understand the "why" and how it has served their successes. Every instruction, course of action, and desired result must start with a decision. The researcher's automobile assembly line story puts this into perspective. The leaders that understood why the doors needed to fit by design, not by default.

Not all leaders created the company allowing them to focus on building organizational culture from the ground up. When leaders assume a position within an established company, they can utilize tactics to assess the culture and make the beginning of the building process start with them and with what they determine is the "why" for the organization. Sinek (2009) determined leaders facing challenges in today's world, getting more out of fewer people and fewer resources, can be successful by building a company that recruits employees that all fit the organization based upon the original intention and goal. Ensuring the right people are in the organization by knowing the people, knowing what they value and believe, and how employees believe the company can always be seeking improvement (Bryant, 2011).

Leadership and organizational culture intersect in the arena of human influence. Sinek (2009) determined there are two ways to influence human behavior: manipulate it or inspire it. The author utilized the idea of carrots and sticks to provide clarity in his research of human behavior. Manipulations can drive a sale, like transactional leadership, but not create loyalty among employees. In contrast, inspirational leaders, or transformational leaders, can rally employees not for a single event, but for years. The concept of fear in creating and sustaining organizational culture has been an area of focus for this researcher. When fear is employed, facts are incidental and uses an analogy of terrorism to articulate fear in organizations. It is not the statistical probability that a person could get hurt by a terrorist, it is the fear it might happen that cripples a population. Inspiration is the means to create and sustain organizational culture and health. Manipulation is described in the terrorism analogy. Sinek (2009) attests you can get someone to buy a gym membership with manipulation and an aspirational message, but to get them to go there three days a week requires inspiration. The testament of why an organization exists lies in the leader understanding, clarifying, and living that why as a model behavior for the rest of the people in the organization. The ability to manage people is attributed to being fair, honest, and direct in a helpful way similar to a coach leading an athletic team versus simply being a critic of his or her athletes (Bryant, 2011).

These examples of organizational culture research and application to modern companies and modern leaders draw from the foundational research of culture creation. Each author's research provides insight for leaders to utilize in today's world. As mentioned earlier in the chapter, each of the styles represented by Lencioni, Brown, and Sinek are multi-disciplinary and applicable to a variety of companies, organizations, and teams. Implementation of culture changing initiatives can begin at any level of an organization. It is the leader's responsibility to own the narrative and work to communicate from the inside of the organization out (Sinek, 2009). Elements of organizational culture like communication, personalities of employees and leaders, and levels of emotional intelligence can positively impact overall organizational culture with attentiveness from the leaders.

The Influence and Impact of Leadership on Organizational Culture

An organization's culture develops from its leaders. In contrast, the culture can also impact the development of the leadership. Culture building is an element of leadership deemed as important as tactical and strategic thinking within organizations (Bass & Avolio, 1993). The authors attested organizational cultures are often creations of their founders where they shape culture with shared values and assumptions guided by his or her personal beliefs. In a leaders' quest to maintain organizational viability and effectiveness lies strategy and culture (Groysberg et al., 2018). Strategy is evident as a clear focus on goals and decision-making initiatives for the good of the company. Culture can be elusive if it is relegated to be a human resource department function or a secondary concern for a business. Research from the earliest explorations of human nature can model the impact of culture on a business and determine a company's functionality in good times and trying times (Groysberg et al., 2018).

Significant research has been conducted on elements of building and sustaining an organizational culture. Communication within the organization, personalities of leaders and employees, and leadership styles can impact efforts to build a positive organizational culture. When impactful elements of organizational culture are properly aligned it can create energy towards a shared purpose, and the result is an organization with a capacity to thrive (Groysberg et al., 2018).

To provide an understanding of leadership and the relationship to organizational culture, leadership theory sets the platform for organization and implementation of the construct (Sethuraman & Suresh, 2014). No style or theory is considered universal with each utilizing a different approach towards the same goal. A good leader inspires, motivates, and directs activities to achieve organizational goals. An ineffective leader can detract from goal accomplishment and hinder the organizational processes (Amanchukwu et al., 2015). The evolution of leadership styles and theories is a determination that humans are a product of the time and place in which they exist (Hunt & Fedynich, 2018).

Scholars have viewed organizations as social constructions and communication has been recognized as a practice that creates, maintains, and changes organizations (Walker, 2021). Personality research has emerged as an important factor impacting culture. Because employees are a significant asset for all companies, conflict will arise. Leaders can understand their own personalities and those of their employees to sustain a competitive advantage (Syed et al., 2018). The Enneagram has been researched as a practical tool with value for developing transformative leaders and building organizational culture. Understanding self and others creates relationships and shapes understanding and function in healthy organizations (Singletary, 2020).

Shein's (1983) model of organizational culture as a framework determined an organizational culture depends on a definable organization, in the sense of several people interacting with each other for the purpose of accomplishing some goal in their environment. The researcher defined organizational culture as a pattern of basic assumptions a given group has invented, discovered, or developed in learning to cope with problems of external adaptation and internal integration. Those patterns of assumptions that have worked well enough to be considered valid are implemented by being taught to new members as the correct way to perceive, think, and feel in relation to external and internal problems. The foundation of an organization's culture begins with the founder (Schein, 1983).

An organization's founder creates a group and by force of his or her personality, begins to shape the culture. The founders' beliefs, values, and assumptions provide a visible model for how the organization should function (Schein, 1983). Culture manifests itself within three fundamental levels. Those levels are observable artifacts, values, and basic underlying assumptions. Founders and subsequent leaders embed their assumptions and beliefs, but the learning process of organizational culture becomes shared and becomes the total group's experience over time (Schein, 1990). Organizational culture does not develop until the group has overcome crises of growth, worked out solutions for various problems, and created a workable set of rules (Schein, 1983). Basic assumptions was the term utilized to describe rules a group has invented, discovered, or developed in learning to cope with its problems of external adaptation and internal integration. From the process of basic assumptions, culture perpetuates and reproduces itself through the socialization of new members entering the group (Schein, 1990).

Attentiveness to the creation of a valuable, positive culture is the duty of the founder and subsequent leader (Schein, 1990). Utilizing the model of basic assumptions and beliefs, an organization must determine if it possesses a valuable, rare, and imitable culture (Barney, 1986). In research conducted by Mamantha and Geetanjali (2020) a case study analysis into the culture of Apple and its leader, Steve Jobs, determined Jobs' autocratic leadership style characterized as visibly strong and focused, created a culture of employees knowing what was expected out of their projects with criticism from the founder. The company was successful, and the founder determined the working culture and processes in a direct and critical display of beliefs, values, and assumptions.

Schein (1990) determined external adaptation included a mission and primary tasks, specific goals of the organization, the basic means used to accomplish goals, measurement criteria, and remedies if goals are not achieved. Internal integration was determined to be the common language to be used and basic concepts of time and space. Group boundaries, criteria for inclusion, and criteria for allocation of status, power, and authority encompassed internal processes. Other aspects of internal integration were criteria for friendship and love in work settings, and allocation of rewards and punishments. The researcher determined culture descriptions of external adaptations and internal adaptations were best presented by extracts from case studies summarized to illustrate the distinctions between artifacts, values, and assumptions.

To explore organizational culture, researchers must learn about concepts such as climate, norms, and attitudes (Schein, 1990). Analysis of the culture of an organization must focus on three fundamental levels at which culture manifests. Schein's (1990) organizational culture research determined the three levels are observable artifacts, values, and basic underlying assumptions. A paradigm model that illustrates external and internal tasks as means of understanding the organization. Figure 2 displays Schein's organizational culture model retrieved from Gerras et al. (2008).

Figure 2

Illustration of Schein's Model of Organizational Culture

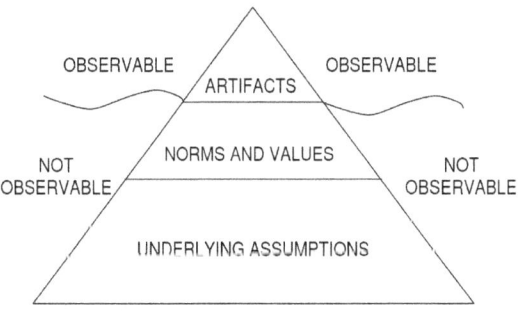

Note. This figure was obtained from Gerras et al. (2008).

Researchers have utilized Schein's model of organizational culture since his research began in the 1980's. Burkus (2014) determined artifacts are the overt and obvious elements of an organization. Artifacts are those things an outsider can see, such as furniture and office layout, dress norms, foosball tables, and free food. Easily observable and visible, artifacts are the first impression of an organization, its surroundings, require further inquiry to understand. To describe Schein's determination of an artifact, Burkus (2014) utilized the example of a company with an airplane wing jutting out from a wall. If one did not understand the culture of the organization, they would need to inquire about the airplane wing to learn the artifact displays a culture of playful experimentation and free expression.

Espoused values are the next layer of Schein's (1990) model of organizational culture. An organization's declared set of values and norms affect how members interact and represent the organization (Burkus, 2014). Public declarations are often used to express core values, statements, or common phrases individuals repeat often. The researcher further defined espoused values with an example of Herb Kelleher, found of Southwest Airlines. Kelleher's was famous for responding to a variety of questions and proposals from colleagues with the phrase "low-cost airline" to reaffirm and reinforce the espoused value of affordability within the Southwest Airlines organization.

Schein's (1990) model declared basic underlying assumptions as the third fundamental level of organizational culture. Burkus (2014) defined the basic assumptions as the essence of culture and the plumb line that values and artifacts square themselves against. Basic underlying assumptions are the bedrock of organizational culture. Assumptions include beliefs and behaviors deeply embedded within the organization. An example from Burkus (2014) related to basic assumptions is Zappos customer service. Zappos focus on providing outstanding customer service to create loyal customers is displayed in their practice of sending potential customers to other retailers if Zappos doesn't have the item in stock. Basic assumptions are manifested in a variety of ways. If assumptions do not align with values, the results are detrimental to the organization and its culture. Another example utilized by Burkus (2014) to describe assumptions was Enron's 64-page manual that outlined the company's mission and values. Enron had values and a mission statement, but the beliefs and behaviors, their basic assumptions, of their accounting practices were not aligned. Enron did not create or sustain a positive organizational culture.

    Schein (1990) determined the strength of an organization's culture is related to the degree of internal consistency within the culture. Internal consistency is a function of the stability of the group, the length of time the group has existed, the intensity of the group's experiences of learning, the mechanisms by which the learning has taken place, and the strength and clarity of the assumptions held by the founders and leaders of group. The researcher also noted any definable group with a shared history can have a culture and within organizations there can be subcultures. Founders and leaders have a duty to understand the scope of cultures and subcultures within organizations. If an organization has had shared experiences, there will be an organizational culture that exists in totality. Further noted, within any given unit, the tendency for integration and consistency creates the possibility for coexisting units of a larger system to have cultures independent and sometimes conflicting with each other. Schein's (1983) foundational model of organizational culture centered around artifacts, values, and basic underlying assumptions created a guide for researchers, organization founders, and leaders to determine the characteristics of an organization's culture.

Leader Communication

Numerous studies have examined communication skills necessary for employers and employees deemed essential within the workplace. Cofflet et al. (2019) attested communication skills are divided into four modes: written, oral, visual, and electronic. The interpretations of types of communication vary among researchers and evidence of society's impact on styles positively and negatively impacts workplace culture. In a study done by the human resources unit at Google, the "people operations department", employees found communication was central to building successful, high-functioning teams at Google (Gallo, 2018). They determined psychological safety was one of the most important qualities found in winning teams. The author noted that the Google research project determined the communication amongst team members, a willingness to speak up, and a safe place to bring diverse ideas to share were actions promoting psychological safety.

Leader communication has been deemed one of the most valuable leadership skills because the impact, positive or negative, resonates with employees and ultimately impacts organizational culture (Hicks, 2020). A health care industry study on communication found leaders must seek to find clarity, actively listen, and use communication to develop relationships. Leaders must understand communication's impact on organizational culture, conflict management, employee satisfaction, and employee retention. Each of those outcomes impact employees and the second order effect is the impact on the customers, the patients, within the health care industry (Hicks, 2020).

Communication research related to organizational culture focuses on feedback as an essential tool for leaders. Feedback is defined as a regulatory mechanism where the effect of an action is fed back to modify and improve future action (Ramani et al., 2019). Various forms of feedback are utilized within organizations in the form of positive or negative feedback. Regardless of feedback type, research indicates people reject feedback if they doubt its credibility (Ramani et al., 2019). Therefore, leaders must be attuned to building relationships with a focus on positive culture, so feedback becomes an impactful growth opportunity for leaders and followers and the overall health of the organization.

Social communication networks within organizations have proven to be of value to culture building. An example of research related to social involvement in organizations is a study produced by Elkins et al. (2011) in which they explored the concept of participation in campus recreational activities associated with a sense of campus community. They found that participation in activities outside of their daily academic routines created a strengthened social network, which impacted their overall sense of community and success.

An element of communication impacting organizational culture that does not involve the leader or leadership is the communication amongst employees. In an ethnographic study of Latina nannies in Los Angeles, California, Armenta (2009) determined a strong sense of community, belonging, support, and socialization was found amongst domestic employees. Within their household work environments, they had different employers or leaders, but they found a community and social space to create community, to reinforce group values, and communicate and work as a team to support one another during their work hours.

Domestic work is often characterized by being socially isolating with low-wage labor positions and social inequalities within households and neighborhoods (Armenta, 2009). The author's research determined the characteristics that separated domestic workers from their employers were the ones that served as the foundation of their informal ties with one another. Functioning much like an organization that was lacking health, culture, and values, the nannies created an organizational culture amongst themselves to provide a foundation for their workspace, the park. The Latina nannies created a source of community life by working at the park. They regularly spent time together, shared care work, and they shared food further illustrating the culture they created in their community life at the park. They had a potluck style lunch each Wednesday and befriended the park staff as part of their community. The author noted the familiarity and friendly interactions between the park staff and the nannies created a mood contributing to the sense of organizational culture in the park. The employees of the park and the domestic employees communicated to the researcher that they felt like a family. Without consistent, formal leadership structure or organizational structure, the Latina nannies created and sustained a positive organizational culture for themselves. The benefit of the creation and sustainability of the culture was intended for the group of nannies and park employees. However, the positive aspects resonated with the families that employed them and the children they cared for (Armenta, 2009).

Communication between leaders and followers, leaders and other leaders, and employee to employee communication all play a significant role in overall organizational culture. Attributes of communication impacting culture are anchored in unspoken behaviors, mindsets, and social patterns and must be attended to be leadership for continuity and growth of the organization (Groysberg et al., 2018).

Personality of the Organization, Leadership, and Employees

Past research has centered around leadership styles and impact of effectiveness on followers and organizations. Research remains consistent from the perspective that leaders serve as the catalyst for culture creation and culture change (Groysberg et al., 2018). Personality is usually thought of as a characteristic of an individual, but Lencioni (2012) defined a company's personality by their values. The researcher asserted the importance of values that create clarity and provide employees clear direction about how to behave. Good values recruit and retain employees because they communicate the personality of the organization and naturally attract the right employees and repel the wrong ones (Lencioni, 2012). Companies should ask the question, "How do we behave?" as a starting point for values and company personality. Creation of and adherence to core values preserves the essence of the organization and not only establishes and sustains a personality for the organization and its employees but attracts customers with similar values. Another perspective related to company personality through values is to keep core values simple, measurable, and minimal. Lencioni (2012) determined too many values dilute the personality and states the organization wants to be a little bit of everything. The values must be measurable, attainable, and relatable to goals and objectives. If core values are broad and read like a marketing phrase, they are not serving a sincere purpose to define personality and behaviors within the organization. They simple become words that leaders and employees to do put to action and create discontent due to unsustainability and applicability daily.

Research related to company personality, values, and effectiveness determines the types of people hired by the organization. Research has broadened the scope of assessment of leaders and followers by learning about their personalities and the impact of personality on organizational structure, effectiveness, and culture (Singletary, 2020). Every organization consists of leaders and employees that must work together as a collection of individuals with a focus on common goals. A personality assessment that was created centuries ago, the Enneagram, is an ancient philosophic approach to human development based upon a nine-pointed pattern (Alonzo, 2000). Each of the nine types details a reflection of patterns of thought, feeling, and action. Personality assessments articulate what is important to an individual and how that individual interacts with the world like the core values of a company's personality (Lencioni, 2012). In the case of an organizational setting, the Enneagram can be used as a resource to understand employees, motivate a work force, be of great value (Alonzo, 2000). Further, it is believed to reveal unconscious motivations that determine human behavior.

The Enneagram's nine types provide insight into how people think, feel, and behave. Lapid-Bogda (2006) conducted a study on leadership training and described Enneagram styles. The Enneagram Style One is the perfectionist. That style is described as people who seek a perfect world to improve themselves and everyone and everything around them, the pursuit of excellence. Style Two is characterized as giving. Individuals categorized as style two want to be liked and meet the needs of others. Style Three are performers who organize their lives to achieve specific goals to gain respect and admiration of others. Style Four is characterized by individualistic, or dramatic personalities. Those individuals desire deep connections with other people and want to express their feelings in an authentic way. Enneagram Style Five are intellectual people seeking information and knowledge while remaining introverted. Style Six is determined to be one who is loyal but lacks self-confidence. They are prone to worry and plan for the worst-case scenario. Style Seven are those that crave creativity and are spontaneous always keeping options open. Enneagram Style Eight defines those that pursue the truth, are strong, influential, and want to make things happen. Style Nine are individuals that seek peace, harmony, and avoid conflict.

Singletary (2020) determined the Enneagram was a valuable tool for leaders, leadership training, and organizational culture building. Leadership is more than having a role or title and managers do more than manage people. Every person within an organization has the capacity to add value. The author found using the Enneagram in the workplace can affect communication styles, motivation, time management, negotiation, and training and development. The Enneagram provides clarity for employees on how coworkers may approach their actions, thoughts, and feelings within the organization. The author utilized a chart to categorize Enneagram types into subcategories of head, heart, and hand.

From a leadership standpoint, one's Enneagram type provides insight into leadership strengths and help individuals understand weaknesses as well (Lapid-Bogda, 2006). The assessment determines one Enneagram type that is said to remain consistent throughout an individual's lifetime. When used by Lapid-Bogda (2006) in a practical research study within a pharmaceutical company, she determined knowing and using the Enneagram at work as a self-responsibility and self-development tool was reinforced daily. Leaders, managers, and employees used the personality assessment to better understand one another and improve overall communication positively impacting the culture of participation throughout the pharmaceutical company.

The Enneagram provides individuals with an invitation to self-observation that benefits themselves and their organization (Singletary, 2020). Self-observation provides emotional, intellectual, and instinctual elements of personality. Those centers of human functioning create clarity within a workplace setting and encourage a transformative approach to leadership impacting overall organizational culture. Schein's (1990) research determined culture creation centered around how individuals within a group solved problems both externally and internally. The deepest levels of culture creation and growth stemmed from learning in a behavioral, cognitive, and emotional fashion individually and collectively. The result of knowing, understanding, and facilitating communication within an organization allows culture to

overcome invincible structural barriers of an era and transform the behavior of entire industries and social systems (Horowitz, 2019).

Followership and Building Teams

Teams increasingly are being relied upon to accomplish work in corporations and a wide variety of other organizations (Sitkin & Hackman, 2011). Defining and recognizing the unique contributions individuals make that bring strength to a team is a valuable practice for leaders of organizations (Brown, 2018). Brown's (2018) research on building teams centered around building trust. A metaphor for trust building amongst team members was "the marble jar". The researcher indicated effective team building was visible with each person acquiring a jar. When team members, leaders, co-workers showed support, kindness, and honesty, one would put a marble in their jar. When team members showed a lack of support, kindness, or honesty, a marble was removed from their jar. Over time, team members developed trust with marbles as indicators of teamwork and team building. As each member accumulated or lost marbles, trust was impacted. Building teams and followership through strong social cohesion has been shown to build trust between team members with significant impact on organizational culture (Choi et al., 2019).

Principles of Followership

In every professional role in life there is a mixture of leadership and followership. It is essential that every person who has been labeled a leader recognizes the elements of followership in their role (Stern, 2021). Northouse (2019) defined leadership as a process whereby an individual influences a group of individuals. Followership was categorized as important as leadership because one cannot have leaders without followers. Stern (2021) noted in everyone there is a leader and a follower. Followers must recognize amid following they should be attentive to ethical leadership and what the follower should expect from a leader. It is a mutually exclusive relationship.

A case utilized in Northouse (2019) to articulate organizational culture gone wrong in leader and follower dynamics is the Pennsylvania State University sexual abuse scandal of 2008. Joe Paterno, the famed head football coach at Pennsylvania State University, built his brand of coaching around football excellence and academic integrity. As the leader of the organization, he used words such as success and honor to describe his football program. In 2008, the mother of a young man reported her son was sexually abused by a long-time assistant football coach in Paterno's program. An investigation determined other employees within the organization knew of the sexual abuse incidents and failed to report them because they feared for their jobs and their futures. The power of the head coach, the football program, and its reputation hindered the followers from acting in an ethical manner. The author concluded the lesson from the case study was a focus on how the dynamics of followers and leaders impacted the failures within their organizational culture. In the end, their failures impacted the lives of many young men and tarnished the reputation of Pennsylvania State University and its football program.

Kipfelsberger and Kark (2018) conducted a study on leader meaningfulness and its impact on followers. The researchers determined most literature utilized the dominant perspective of leaders as a positive influence. The authors noted people across generations, particularly today's emerging workforce born after 1980, are motivated to realize their selves at work and focus on opportunities that will enhance their personal sense of meaningfulness. Using the perspective of top-down, bottom-up, and leaders and followers as agents, Kipfelsberger and Kark (2018) determined meaningful work in organizations consists of coherence, purpose, and significance. Coherence refers to an employees' understanding and ability to make sense of what is happening at work. Purpose is the directionality of employees' work and the ability to connect their work to a higher-order goal. Significance is an employees' evaluation of their worth in the context of their work. Within this study, the researchers concluded followers' sense of meaning and their need for meaning is an aspect of organizational life impacting organizational culture. Leaders' attentiveness to the perspective of followers is a responsibility to sustain meaningfulness in the workplace.

Sitkin and Hackman (2011) interviewed Duke University's renowned basketball coach, Mike Krzyzewski, to obtain insights, experience, and advice on leading teams.

Coach Krzyzewski noted sometimes the best leaders are the youngest and newest members of the team. The need for team members to commit to and be part of the culture as followers had a significant impact on the creation and sustainability of the Duke University Men's Basketball culture. Coach Krzyzewski determined one of his most important duties as a leader was to help individual players excel. In teaching individuals how to excel, he also helped everyone learn how to help teammates. From the interview, the authors concluded creating followers of the Duke University Men's Basketball philosophy and culture included building teams, and building relationships in a positive, sustainable way.

Building Teams

Lencioni (2012) stated teamwork is not a virtue, it is a strategic choice. Often misunderstood as a working group or committee, a team of people willing to accept work and make sacrifices will function as a team with the intentional decision to do so. To further articulate the difference between a working group or committee and a team, Lencioni (2012) used a sports analogy. A working group or committee is like a golf team where each players goes and plays on their own and they add up their scores at days end. A team functions like a basketball team, a team that plays together simultaneously, mutually dependent upon one another to achieve their goal of winning basketball games.

To understand the dynamic of building teams to create, maintain, and sustain organizational culture, research on leadership styles provides insight on leader and employee interactions related to creating teams for the proposed outcome or goal. The research of Bass and Avolio determined three dominant leadership styles (Echevarria et al. 2016). The leadership styles from the research included transformational leadership, transactional leadership, and laissez-faire leadership. Leaders display a dominant tendency to display one of the three leadership styles (Echevarria et al., 2016). Laissez-faire leadership is essentially defined as a non-leader (Kirkbride, 2006). Laissez-faire is a French phrase for "let it be" (Amanchukwu, 2015). Researchers determined this leadership style can allow team members significant autonomy and increase job satisfaction or be damaging to subordinates with poor time management.

Bass et al. (1996) determined four components of transformational leadership: charismatic, inspirational, intellectually stimulating, and individually considerate. They contrast transformational styles with transactional leadership including components of management-by-exception and contingent reward. The researchers defined the third leadership style, laissez-faire, as non-leadership, and avoidance of leadership.

The strength of determining and understanding leadership styles is the application to a wide variety of organizations. A study by Toor & Ofori (2009) examined ethical leadership in Singapore's construction industry. Their findings indicted a positive and significant relationship between ethical leadership and transformational leadership. In a study of a private business in Kosovo, research determined transformational leadership is receiving more attention because it increases focus on employees' spontaneous awareness and self-confidence to raise overall morale and levels of motivation within the organization (Lokaj & Sadrija, 2020).

Research related to transformational, transactional, and laissez-faire leadership has also been used by researchers to study the impact of leaders on athletic teams or sport programs. In Sitkin and Hackman's (2011) article about Duke University's Men's Basketball coach, Mike Krzyzewski, the coach dedicated his transformational leadership style to the stability of his assistant coaches, and the support of his leaders, the President, and Athletic Director at Duke University. McCann et al. (2015) found prior research using the model was primarily found within businesses and in the military. The researchers studied the leader behaviors of college soccer coaches and determined transformational leadership had a positive relationship with team effectiveness, transactional leadership had an insignificant relationship with effectiveness, and laissez-faire leadership produced negative relationships with extra efforts, but a positive relationship with satisfaction among team members.

    The impact of leader styles on building teams is applicable to a variety of settings from business to military, and athletics. The factors of leadership as displayed on a continuum from transformational leadership to passive leadership are easy to understand and apply in a practical manner as presented in previous paragraphs (McCann et al., 2015). Research developed throughout the years allowed Bruce Avolio and Bernard Bass the ability to identify behaviors associated with each of the three styles (Arenas et al., 2017). Leader behaviors associated with each leadership style serves as a guide for implementation and understanding of team members to achieve desired outcomes within the organization. The research of Arenas et al. (2017) provides modern day characteristics associated with each style as an outline and overview for learning and understanding styles and their application to building teams.

    The transformational leadership style behaviors include individual consideration, intellectual stimulation, inspirational motivation, and idealized influence. The key component is for leaders to motivate their followers to accomplish more than intended and reach their full potential. A focus on creating personal relationships with followers in meaningful resulting in increasing their levels of motivation and morality (Arenas et al., 2017). Individual consideration is characterized by a leader coaching, mentoring, actively listening, and valuing diversity. Intellectual stimulation facilitates innovative thinking and efforts to reframe old problems. Inspirational motivation is when a leader motivates, inspires, and articulates a vision for the organization. Idealized influence is when the leader is a role model, well-respected, admired, and has high ethical standards.

The transactional leadership behaviors are categorized as management by exception, either passive or active, and contingent reward. Arenas et al. (2017) characterized management by exception (passive) when a leader responds to deviations in standards only when necessary. Management by exception (active) is when a leader responds to deviations in standards as soon as possible. Contingent reward is a leader behavior characterized by rewarding followers for performance.

The laissez-faire leadership style is characterized as a leader's avoidance or absence of leadership due to the hands-off leadership approach encompassed by this style (Arenas et al., 2017). Actions associated with this style include avoidance of decision making, abdication of responsibilities, avoiding taking stands on issues, and non-development of followers.

The influence of leaders in building teams through transformational, transactional, or passive leadership styles is of value to researchers of organizational culture. In a study of teamwork and collaboration in hospital and healthcare institutions, researchers determined a major significant relationship between teamwork and collaboration and building an effective learning organizational culture (Alonazi, 2021).

Values

Frontiera (2010) described organizational culture as the values that hold an organization together. Dempsey (2015) noted a corporate culture was the intrinsic values shared by organization members that underpin organizational goals. When group members enter a joint commitment to share certain values, they are doing so beyond making it common knowledge. Group members determine they will endorse the same values, display a commitment, and decide values and commitment together. Joint commitments related to creating and accepting values in corporate culture develops a shared understanding of how a group will proceed as a unit together for good of the organization.

Brown (2018) conducted research about leaders, deemed daring leaders, and how they incorporated values into their work and organizations. Values, a way of being or believing held most important, required work and contemplation to define. Living into values as an action of a leader means he or she does more than profess values. Those values are practiced. When values are clear, leaders can articulate what they believe with intentions, words, thoughts, and behaviors guided by living those values. In research conducted by this author with over ten thousand organizational leaders, facilitated workshops were implemented on creating and determining values. From a significant list of choices, participants were encouraged to select two values for their organizations. The researcher discovered most organizational leaders were inclined to select ten or fifteen values for their organizations. Participants were required to select two values most fitting for their leadership and their organization. A long list of values was indicative that nothing was important because everything was listed as important. Two was determined the essential number of values because they served as a flashlight, to help organizations find their way in the dark. Two values simply defined what was most important and dear to the organization and the leaders of the organization. Brown (2018) concluded two values had the capacity to fill an organization with purpose.

Values are a significant contributor in the overall development and sustainability of organizational culture (Schein, 1990). As Brown's (2018) research indicated, creation of values is essential for leaders of organizations. Beyond determination of values, implementation was profoundly impactful for organizations. Brown (2018) found only about 10 percent of organizations have operationalized their values into teachable and observable behaviors used to train employees and impact accountability. The research determined an unwillingness to translate values into behaviors is indicative of leaders not teaching people the skills they need to create a culture and hold one another accountable. Schein's model of organizational culture determined values are part of the cultural foundation by giving meaning to the daily activities and work of a group or organization (Schein & Schein, 2017).

To understand the importance of values, Brown's (2018) research utilized a practical approach for leaders of organizations to develop, implement, and hold members accountable for organizational values. The researcher noted a process of living into values was successful for members to be accountable and hold others accountable. Living into values was done so by defining supporting behaviors, those behaviors aligned with organizational values. And, clarification of slippery behaviors, those actions that are tempting, but do not align values. The author concluded if leaders and organizations do not make values priorities, they cannot ask others to do so.

Communication Methods within Organizations

Understanding the dynamics of office communication often equates to knowing the unwritten rules of how to communicate in a particular office setting. Communication norms are learned and reinforced by colleagues (Dhawan, 2021). Schein (1993) utilized the term, dialogue, to describe a fundamental human skill necessary for organizations and organizational culture. To understand the importance of dialogue, is to accept its role in the facilitation and creation of new possibilities for valid communication. Groups, teams, and organizations that make dialogue the root of action facilitate common ground and mutual trust. From that common ground and trust is the ability to really speak about what is on one's mind (Schein, 1993).

Historically, research on communication methods in the workplace was written from the standpoint of face-to-face communication via meetings, group discussions, and leader/subordinate exchanges (Schein, 1993). With a significant increase in hybrid work, a combination of in-office work and remote work, a need has arisen to implement and understand digital communication within organizations (Dhawan, 2021). In a study conducted by Tran (2017), the author determined Google was a company that constantly experimented to find the best way to satisfy employees and help them work effectively. Communication was a key factor for Google's culture due to its decentralized workforce with integrated units working together to find solutions and prevent failure.

In a study of approximately 2,000 office workers, over 70% experienced some form of unclear communication from their colleagues. The result was the average employee wasted four hours per week on poor, confusing digital communications. Those statistics add up to an average of $188 billion wasted annually across the American economy due to a lack of understanding in digital communications. Digital communications, when utilized properly and incorporated as part of the norms of organizational culture, can be a significant asset to a variety of businesses and business cultures (Dhawan, 2021).

Research conducted by Dhawan (2021) on utilization of electronic communication methods in business, determined email was best utilized to provide directional, important, and timely information. Norms for email include utilizing to share attachments but avoid use when immediate response is required. Email use should be priority dependent. Text messages within organizational communication should be used only when unable to reach someone via other channels. Corporate cultures can determine text messages as a preferred communication between leader and employees. The researcher further attests, as a rule, that form of communication should be priority dependent with a determination on the status of use as a norm. Video calls have been utilized for hybrid work settings and provide the benefits of visual interaction, introductions, visual information sharing in the form of slides or decks, and a means to check-in on projects and ideas. When scheduled in advance, video calls can influence the culture of communication with personal interactions and an ability to record the call if a member is unable to attend.

Establishment of communication processes, procedures, and norms within an organization is essential for leaders and managers. A detailed guide of best practices ensures everyone on a team or within an organization is on the same page with the same expectations regardless of their physical location (Dhawan, 2021). In Trans' (2017) study on Google's culture, the author noted a creative working environment stimulated communication within the workplace. In 2011, Google purchased 100 bicycles for employees to utilize on its sprawling campus to facilitate employee interaction and communication at work. At the time of publishing the study in 2017, Google had a fleet of 1300 brightly colored bikes for employees. Navigating the campus for communication and collaboration became a norm.

Elements of a Startup Culture

Elements of organizational culture in startup companies mirror those of established companies with influences from the company founder or leader. Principles of leadership, values creation, and followership are evident in new and existing companies. The perspectives, focus, and patterns of growth are elements that differentiate startups from established companies. The most impactful difference startup companies, due to the smaller size of the organizations, is everyone has the power to influence, create, and impact the overall culture (Lazarova, 2020).

Burkus (2011) researched Zappos, an online shoe retailer startup, to investigate culture creation and sustainability of a startup. Data from the study found the leadership influence of the founder was significant. Strategies for hiring, onboarding, and finding employees fitting for the culture and values of Zappos were the key to startup culture successes for the online shoe retailer. Lazarova (2020) noted startups foster the demand to grow and hire the best talents naturally. Thus, creating practices to put employees in the center of company growth with the result being work-life balance and additional benefits related to small companies. The company culture becomes the personality of the startup and the employees and is crucial for building leadership teams as the company transitions from startup to middle-sized company.

Ganz (2009) noted the importance of narrative. Each organization has a unique history and story. Startups control the narrative, structure the story, and create principles and values for a sustainable growth pattern for their companies. Apple was once a startup focused on creativity, structuring the narrative, and creating rituals to celebrate team successes and overall company success. Startups, like Apple and Zappos, focused on constant improvement, training employees, and development opportunities influence organizational culture in a positive way (Lazarova, 2020). As noted in Burkus' (2011) study on Zappos as a startup company, the founder consulted with employees over time to establish core values and a mission statement. As a team, within a flat reporting structure, employees and leaders considered culture central to building an ethical organization, supportive of a positive organizational culture. The culture was as a centralized purpose and goal for the company as much so as profits and growth.

Startup companies present opportunities for innovative ideas with a focus on habits and rituals directly related to strengthening the organizational culture and unique narrative. Characterized by small teams, meaningful jobs, and employees seeking to grow and develop with the company, startups establish goals as a cohesive team, and are dedicated to revisions and updates to consistently enhance and support organizational culture (Lazarova, 2020). Startup cultures are not about team outings, unlimited vacation, or free food. It is about treating people right and the willingness to work as a team through growing pains to create and sustain organizational culture (Nordli, 2021).

Summary

To understand organizational culture is to understand the key values, rules of behavior, and assumptions about what is important. The development of a culture is evolutionary. What a group has learned in its efforts to survive, grow, and deal with in its environment forces the group to organize itself. As a social unit with a shared history and a shared learning process comes stability and experiences that are the creation of culture at every stage (Schein & Schein, 2016).

Schein's model of organizational culture determined culture was group learning simultaneously as a behavioral, cognitive, and emotional process (Schein, 1990). The results of learned behaviors, concepts, and understandings led to observable artifacts, values, and basic underlying assumptions that defined the foundation of an organization's culture. From Schein's (1990) cultural levels of artifacts, values, and assumptions, modern researchers implemented variations of the foundation to further understand the creation and sustainability of organizational cultures.

Lencioni (2012) conducted research on organizational health. The determining factor in creation and evolution of a healthy organization was centered around clarity. Clarity of values, behaviors, and initiatives from the leader to other members of the organization was most impactful on organizational health, the status of the organization's culture. Brown's (2018) research focused on the leader of an organization. From a traditional style of armored leadership to a modern, inclusive style of daring leadership, Brown (2018) determined organizational cultures thrive with the understanding being clear is kind and being unclear is unkind. Sinek (2009) determined values, behaviors, and assumptions must center around why. Leaders and organizations that remained focused on their values and the reason why they exist as a company will be more likely to foster a positive organizational culture.

Culture is not a mission statement or a list of values on a wall. It is a strong force of behaviors and actions with a target that is always moving. As conditions shift, strategy evolves, and culture must change accordingly (Horowitz, 2019). Culture is crucial and not defined from a list, but from what leaders and members of an organization do. What you do is who you are (Horowitz, 2019). Chapter three will detail the methods of podcast data collection, document analysis, and survey methods as a means for understanding the organizational culture of a startup company. Culture is created, reenacted, and reinforced through time (Tran, 2017). With modern methods of podcast interviews, the researcher seeks to understand the phenomenon of the organizational culture of a startup athletic apparel company. From its inception as a startup, to its current state of success as a rapidly growing private business, creation of and reinforcement of the culture will be examined from the perspective of the founder, the departmental leaders, and the employees.

Chapter Three: Methodology

Overview

The purpose of this study was to explore how artifacts, norms and values, and underlying assumptions created and reinforced the organizational culture of a startup athletic apparel company (Schein, 2004). The subject of this research study was a startup company based in Los Angeles, California. This study involved emerging questions and data collected in the participant's setting, through company-produced podcasts, to allow the researcher to make interpretations of the meanings within the data related to organizational culture (Creswell, 2014). Data were collected from pre-recorded podcast interviews, document analysis of website content, and email surveys to explore values, behaviors, and communication practices within the organization. The researcher aimed understand how defined values within the organization contributed to trust and the overall creation and sustainability of the organizational culture. This chapter details the study design, scope, and procedures utilizing a case study format to explore the organizational culture of a startup athletic apparel company.

Design

A qualitative case study method using interview data from podcasts, document analysis, and email surveys was utilized to answer the research questions. Case study research design utilizes an approach that facilitates an exploration of a phenomenon within its context using a variety of sources (Creswell, 2014). Qualitative design allowed the researcher to ensure the topic of interest, organizational culture, is well explored through various data collection methods worthy of discussion (Baxter & Jack, 2008). The essence of the defined values, norms, and communication within the subject company was revealed as each method is employed within the context of exploring the facets of organizational culture. Schein (1990) determined it was not possible to provide complete descriptions of organizational culture within journal articles. Instead, extracts from cases could be summarized to illustrate the distinctions between artifacts, values, and assumptions. The researcher determined a case study design with triangulation of data from podcasts, document analysis, and surveys enabled a thorough review of the organizational culture at the subject startup company.

Research Questions

RQ1: What are the organizational structures and processes that contribute to the creation and sustainability of the organizational culture?

RQ2: What are the values, strategies, and goals that determine the organizational culture at the startup athletic apparel company?

RQ3: What are actions, perceptions, and beliefs within the culture that are mutually reinforced by leaders and employees?

Setting

The setting of this research study is a startup athletic apparel company founded in 2015. The company is based in Los Angeles, California and specializes in selling fun and fashionable sunglasses to active communities of athletes (Biel, 2020). Three avid runners and high school friends developed the brand with the original focus to create running sunglasses that were affordable, yet fashionable and not over-engineered and overpriced (Startup, 2021). Since 2015, the company has expanded its line of eyewear beyond running to other sports like cycling, golf, gaming, and cross-training. The startup sells fashionable, fun, and affordable sunglasses with 1400 retail accounts across 50 countries worldwide and has sold over one million pairs in their short history as an athletic apparel brand (Biel, 2020).

Since its creation, the founders have focused on creating and sustaining a positive organizational culture that complements its brand characteristics. To apply for a job, one must submit a drawing of an octopus fighting a pirate. The founders attested it sets the tone to display an organization that places high value on having fun (Biel, 2020). By employing offbeat onboarding strategies and innovative management strategies, the company focuses on alignment with the company culture in all processes.

The company has grown from a startup created by three friends in 2015 to nearly 100 employees. The company brand has collaborated with major brands, won several awards, and is dedicated to selling fun in the form of athletic eyewear (Startup, 2021). The rapid growth has centered on principals of culture related to setting the tone, an organized onboarding process for employees, productivity as the priority, and innovative management practices (Biel, 2020). From 2015 when the company was founded to 2019, the company increased revenue 300 percent annually (Lease, 2019).

The company founders stated the mission was to give people permission to unabashedly be themselves and exemplify that freedom with a mascot, a flamingo, to display the fun, unique culture of the brand and the company (Startup, 2021). The company has grown rapidly since 2015 and currently has 12 teams, or departments, called the ecosystem. Structured in a traditional way with a startup twist, the organizational chart is a circle versus a traditional top-down chart. Within the ecosystem, or organizational structure, the teams consist of:

- Human resources
- Direct to consumer sales
- Content and copy
- Brand management
- Activations
- Project management
- Distribution center
- Customer service
- Operations
- Finance
- Product development
- Sales

Company founders attested their ecosystem is an ever evolving, living, breathing, thing with each team member having an essential job to do. Organizations are social fields where complex information and knowledge are produced and communicated amongst humans (Mills et al., 2001). The startup company founders and leaders have focused on the sales success of their fun brand while systematically focusing on the employees. The focus is on creating an organizational culture that mimics the brand with fun and success. This organization was selected for this study because was a startup company and the leaders have focused on creating and sustaining a positive organizational culture since the beginning in 2015 (Startup, 2021).

Like Google and Zappos, this startup shares the same point of establishing an organizational culture to bring the best for their employees. Zappos, formerly a startup company led by Tony Hsieh, focused on culture from its beginnings as on online shoe retailer. Hsieh is quoted as stating "your culture is your brand" (Tran, 2017). Further, although Google conducts business in a different setting, the company focus is on building a workforce which reflects and understands the needs of all employees similar to the subject company.

Participants

The participants in this case study were current employees of the startup athletic apparel company. The founder and current Chief Executive Officer, each of the departmental leaders, and employees within each of the departments were included in the study. The case study methodology allowed the researcher to explore the organizational culture phenomenon through various data sources and a variety of lenses to reveal multiple facts of the phenomenon (Baxter & Jack, 2008).

Researchers have determined organizational cultures primarily reflect their leaders. Leaders influence culture through their strategies, values, and practices (Steers & Shim, 2013). The participants in this study categorized as the leaders include the founder and Chief Executive Officer. In addition to leaders, one or more influential group members can have a significant positive or negative influence on the culture of a group (Warrick, 2017). Participants in this study included departmental leaders of each of the 12 departments. The third area of participants included employees not serving in formal leadership positions. At the time of the study, the company founder determined there were 80 employees serving in non-leadership positions. Exploring the perspective of employees that are not founders or departmental leaders provided an understanding of their perceptions of the cultural norms and practices. Warrick (2017) described a strong culture as one with a clear understanding of the cultural values and norms are. Weak culture was described as one with confusing or inconsistent norms and practices. Exploration of the phenomenon of culture at three levels of the organization's structure provided a comprehensive view of the norms, artifacts, and assumptions at this startup company as they relate to Schein's (2004) foundation of organizational culture.

Sampling

The entire population of employees, approximately 93, were included in the study. The podcast interview data included interviews with the founders and current leaders of each department within the company. A total of 18 podcasts were analyzed for this study. Podcasts used for this case study were produced and made available by the subject company. The researcher listened to all podcasts produced by the subject company. From the catalog of podcasts, the researcher analyzed the ones specifically related to the topic of organizational culture. The specification of podcasts related to organizational culture resulted in inclusion of six podcast interviews with the founders and current Chief Executive Officer related to company culture and culture creation. Data were analyzed based upon the research questions. Additionally, 12 podcast interviews, one with each department leader, were analyzed for this study. Those 12 interviews included the entire available catalog of organizational culture podcasts with departmental leaders. Thus, the total number of podcasts analyzed for the case study resulted in 18. Podcasts produced by the subject company provided the researcher the ability to collect direct evidence, deemed essential for a case study (Yin, 2009).

Document analysis was not limited to certain employees or departments. An overall analysis of website information and content was comprehensive and included all available website data related to organizational culture available at the time of the study. The document analysis encompassed job postings, the mission statement, values statement, photos, videos, and quotes. Document analysis excluded product data and pricing on the website as irrelevant to the study.

A stratification of employee-participants was employed for the online survey data collection. The researcher administered the survey via Qualtrics to the entire population of employees not serving in formal leadership positions. The researcher, from data provided by the company founder, estimated at the time of the study, 80 employees were categorized as the population for this aspect of the study. Data from founders, departmental leaders, and employees in non-leadership positions provided a comprehensive study of the organizational culture at a startup athletic apparel company.

Procedures

The case study method involves a range of empirical material collection tools to answer the research questions with maximum breadth (Rashid et al., 2019). The case study approach was utilized to discover processes involved in value cocreation. The goal of case study research is to discover patterns containing evidence of collaboration among participants, or employees, which emerge after documentation and thoughtful interpretation of the empirical data (Rashid et al., 2019).

This case study on the organizational culture of a startup athletic apparel company, began with the researcher securing approval from the company's Chief Executive Officer. The researcher requested approval to conduct each element of the study on the company including podcast data collection, document analysis, and email surveys. Rashid et al. (2019) determined seeking permission in a timely manner is one of the most important steps in qualitative research. Clarification and approval from the startup were followed by the researcher seeking approval from the Institutional Review Board (IRB) to conduct the research study.

A hallmark of case study research is the use of multiple sources to enhance data credibility (Yin, 2003). First, podcast data was used as interview data collection. The subject startup company had a podcast series specifically dedicated to the subject of organizational culture. The podcasts were available to the public via the internet. However, for ethical consideration, the researcher requested approval from the subject company to use the podcasts for this study. The podcasts included interviews with company founders and departmental leaders dedicated to the subject of organizational culture. The importance of using interviews was to generate themes, theories, and models directly from the source, company founders and leaders (Paradis et al., 2016). The interviews included employee perspectives related to the efforts and focus on organizational culture within each department at the startup. The podcast series utilized for this element of the study were produced by the subject company and featured company founders as the interviewers and interviewees. Other interviewees were the department heads, or flock leaders, as they are called at this company. A qualitative design with podcast data provided specific interview data to examine the organizational culture of the startup company from the perspective of the founders of the company and the departmental leaders.

Second, document analysis was utilized to seek themes on the company website. Creswell (2014) noted document analysis enables a researcher to obtain language and words of participants that represents data to which participants have given attention.

Website data was collected and analyzed by the researcher. Document analysis allowed the researcher to determine themes, match patterns of communication, and link data related to organizational culture (Baxter & Jack, 2008). This method of data collection has been described as creative by Creswell (2014) because it enables to the researcher to obtain language, videos, pictures, and words of participants. Document analysis of website data captured visual attention as a communication method for the organization's leaders and employees (Creswell, 2014). Utilization of document analysis for data collection encompassed website content, pictures, stories, and videos which ensured the organizational culture of the startup was explored through a variety of lenses. One website, the subject company's site, was analyzed. All content on the website available at the time of the study was analyzed for this element of the research study. The website data encompassed the mission statement, values declarations, job postings, six videos, a variety of stories, and more than 20 photos. The diversity of exploration and research from a variety of lenses allows for multiple facets of the phenomenon to be revealed and understood (Baxter & Jack, 2008).

    The third method of data collection included email surveys administered via Qualtrics that allowed participants to provide information about the organizational culture with the researcher controlling the line of questioning (Creswell, 2014). This study included a survey with demographic questions and open ended questions. Appendix A details survey questions and structure utilized for the study. The survey was administered to employees in non-leadership positions. Or those employees categorized as not currently serving as a company founder or department head position. The surveys expanded the number of participants in the research study and provided the researcher with data from employees working at varying levels of the company's organizational chart. Paradis et al. (2016) attested interviews are ideal when used to document participants' accounts, perceptions of, or stories about attitudes toward and responses to certain situations and phenomena. The open-ended survey questions solicited information in written form about employee accounts, perceptions, and stories.

The Researchers Role

Qualitative research is interpretive with the researcher involved in a sustained and intensive experience with participants (Creswell, 2014). The researcher collected and analyzed non-numerical data to understand concepts, opinions, and experiences of founders, leaders, and employees of a startup athletic apparel company. The researcher first learned of this startup company as a consumer of athletic apparel sold by the company. In a work setting, the researcher previously hosted the Chief Executive Officer (CEO) in a video phone call for a college level leadership studies course. The CEO spoke to college students about the company culture, leadership, and entrepreneurship. Beyond consumer knowledge of the brand and the company and interactions related to coordinating a guest speaker appearance via video at the researcher's workplace, the researcher does not personally know any employees at the startup.

The researcher utilized a constructivist perspective to address the processes of interaction among individuals within the organization (Creswell, 2014). Utilizing podcast interviews, data analysis, and survey methods of data collection, the researcher explored the meanings, views, and interactions of the participants' perspective on the organizational culture at the startup company. This study explored the organizational culture of one startup athletic apparel company with a case study approach. Creswell

(2014) described case study research illustrates an issue and the researcher compiles a detailed description of the setting for the case.

The researcher had previous knowledge of the aspects of the culture at the startup based upon interactions and interpretations as a consumer and within a professional setting. However, to prevent bias, the podcast data and document analysis information are directly organized and administered by company founders and leaders. The researcher did not author the questions for the podcast interviews. Document analysis encompassed a review of website data authored and administered by the subject company. Lastly, the employee survey was written based upon the research questions and the elements of Schein's (1983) framework.

Instruments

Researchers have used the term organizational culture in a broad sense to refer to the culture of a whole organization or any unit of people working together within the organization (Warrick, 2017). Podcasts, document analysis, and surveys were utilized as instruments for this research. The variety of instruments provided a comprehensive case study approach that facilitated exploration of the phenomenon of organizational culture at a startup (Baxter & Jack, 2008).

Podcasts are digital audio programs focused on various topics. They are accessible on the internet, typically as a free download, and have emerged as a popular means to disseminate and consume information (Naff, 2020). Podcasts consisting of interview data created and disseminated by the subject company were used as an instrument for this study. Lundstrom and Lundstrom (2021) noted podcasts were a medium located at the intersection of the digital and nondigital worlds. And a vibrant and transformable field site, suitable for exploration. The podcast series utilized for this study was specifically dedicated to educating listeners about organizational culture within the company. Thus, the podcast series was determined to be a valuable and accessible data collection instrument due to the production of ideas that is ongoing, fluid, and contested, like every day social interactions (Lundstrom & Lundstrom, 2021).

In document analysis of website main pages, photographs, videos, and any forms of sounds or visual material on the website provided the researcher access to information related to the study (Creswell, 2014). Utilizing a thematic approach to document review, the researcher summarized key features of website data as a method for identifying, describing, and reporting themes related to the research questions and organizational culture (Nowell et al., 2017). In a study conducted by English (2020), use of the search engine on the website was utilized to enter terms specific to the study. Review of documents, videos, presentations, and other content related specifically to the study were conducted with a manual search. English (2020) determined thorough document analysis provided sufficient data to bring confidence to the addressing the research question. In this study, theoretically and methodologically sound analysis of website data aims to produce insight, rich, and trustworthy research findings.

The third instrument was an open-ended survey (see Appendix A). Open-ended surveys with questions that are few are intended to elicit views and opinions from the participants (Creswell, 2014). The survey method was used to examine perspectives of employees in non-leadership positions to determine how the organizational culture impacts them personally and professionally. Seeking out objective evidence from employees was important to determine if there are disconnects between leaders' words and actions (Perkins, 2019). As noted in Schein's (1983) model of organizational culture, behaviors are indicative of company culture health and sustainability. Observable behaviors and interpretations of company values are worthy of assessment pertaining to culture (Perkins, 2019). Workplace assessments inquiring about observable behaviors rather than thoughts or motives are of value to understanding employee perspectives (Morell-Samuels, 2002). A portion of survey in Appendix A was adapted from Perkins (2019) article detailing simple assessment recommendations for companies seeking to explore and understand the state of their organization's culture. Demographic questions were included in the survey as well as questions developed from the research questions and Schein's (1983) theoretical framework of organizational culture.

The data collection instruments for this study were aimed to create reader interest, capture useful information, and to stretch the imagination about possibilities beyond traditional qualitative observations and interviews (Creswell, 2014). The accessibility to podcasts and document analysis provides data collection instruments associated modern technologies and the most up-to-date information for the researcher. Baxter and Jack (2008) determined each data instrument is one piece of the puzzle with each piece contributing to the researcher's understanding of the whole phenomenon. Organizational culture is vital to a company's success. Understanding the state of company culture is a prerequisite for consistent improvement (Perkins, 2019). The researcher aimed to utilize podcasts, document analysis, and survey data collection instruments to understand the phenomenon of the organizational culture at a startup athletic apparel company.

Data Collection

Participants for this study were purposefully selected to provide the researcher with data to understand the phenomenon of organizational culture within the company. Case study research has the potential to deal with simple through complex situations. This method of qualitative research enables one to answer how and why a phenomenon exists and the context of influence (Baxter & Jack, 2008).

The researcher gathered data from podcasts, document analysis, and open-ended email surveys. As previously noted, a variety of data collection instruments create interest, capture useful information, and provide the researcher with the timeliest information associated with the participants and subject being studied (Creswell, 2014). The subject company produced a series of podcasts dedicated to organizational culture. The researcher listened to all podcasts in the series and selected podcasts specific to organizational culture. Podcasts chosen for analysis were selected to examine data and further understand the scope of the growth of the company and the attentiveness to culture from the very beginning to its current state. Six podcasts were categorized by the researcher as relevant to the case study due to interview data directly related to creating and sustaining organizational culture within the subject company. Those podcasts included interview data from the CEO and company founders. Twelve additional podcasts, one podcast interview with each of company's departmental leaders, were analyzed for this study to provide a comprehensive examination of the culture from leaders within the company other than the CEO and founders. Therefore, a total of 18 podcasts encompassed the data examined and analyzed for this research study. Podcast data from founders and each of the twelve departmental leaders provided the researcher with insight and information from the top-level administrators related to their influence and impact on organizational culture.

Document analysis included a review of the company website including videos, photos, text, and other forms of sound which might provide stories, narratives, or digital archives related to the study (Creswell, 2014). Job postings, blogs posts, and up-to-date news and information available to the public were included in the analysis. Delimitations for document analysis included data related to culture including values, the mission statement, job postings, organizational structures, and human resources related information. Product descriptions, photos of athletic apparel, and prices were not included for analysis in this study. All pages related to the company, not the products encompassed the document analysis.

The open-ended survey (see Appendix A) with elements adapted from Perkins (2019) article related to simple assessments of organizational culture was administered via Qualtrics to all employees not serving in leadership positions. At the time of the study, approximately 80 employees were in this population. Participation was voluntary in that neither the researcher or the company founders and leaders had influence over employee survey participation. The scope of data collection for the survey method was to expand the perspective beyond founders and leaders to understand the phenomenon of organizational culture at all levels of the organization.

Data Analysis

Data were transcribed and coded to determine how artifacts, norms, values, and assumptions influence the organizational culture at a startup company (Schein, 2004). The researcher collectively analyzed the data from each of the three instruments and sources ensuring data were converged to understand the overall case, contributing factors, and the influences related to organizational culture (Baxter & Jack, 2008). Qualitative research proceeds together with other aspects of the study as it develops (Creswell, 2014). Due to the dense, rich data associated with qualitative case study research, computer data analysis functions and features within Microsoft Office were utilized by the researcher to analyze data.

In the first round of coding, the researcher utilized deductive coding utilizing Schein's (2004) framework of artifacts, norms and values, and underlying assumptions. Saldana (2021) noted deductive coding was recommended when the conceptual framework suggests certain categories or concepts appear in the data. Data were coded and categorized within one of three elements of Schein's (2004) framework. Data were categorized as artifacts, norms and values, or underlying assumptions. Coding data was performed three separate times, one time for each individual element of the framework. Data related to the specific framework element was highlighted within Microsoft Word. The researcher extracted highlighted data from the complete data set and determined themes from the coded data. Examining key words and phrases from the coded data for each element of the framework provided emerging themes for artifacts, values, and assumptions of the subject company culture.

The second round of coding categorized data specific to the culture of the startup company. Specific verbiage, communication, and processes unique to the subject company were the focus using deductive coding. The second round of coding examined communication styles, specific phrases, and mantras, and processes the startup company used to ground their values of fun and authenticity. This round of coding examined unique actions, words, and meanings within the culture used by leaders and employees attributing to the overall organizational culture.

Codes are utilized to find meaning units in words and sentences that convey similar meanings (Graneheim & Lundman, 2004). A method of descriptive coding was used for this study. Descriptive coding is a system of assigning labels to data to summarize in a word or short phrase the topic of a passage of qualitative data (Saldana, 2021). This author described this method of coding provides the researcher with an inventory of topics for indexing and categorizing. Further, descriptive coding was determined to be appropriate for all qualitative studies, and particularly for beginning qualitative researchers.

Podcast data was collected, transcribed, and coded utilizing functions and features of Microsoft Office to examine organizational culture components of values, artifacts, and assumptions within the organization related to Schein's culture framework (Schein, 2004). The data were analyzed to examine the types and styles of communication within the organization to determine how methods impact organizational culture. Values coding was implemented for document analysis information to examine organizational culture components aligned with data collection methods utilized on the podcasts. Saldana (2021) described values coding as a method for understanding cultures, participant experiences, and actions in a case study. The final method of data collection, email surveys administered via Qualtrics, and analyzed utilizing thematic coding related to Schein's (2004) framework. Each method of data collection was associated with one of the elements of Schein's (2004) framework and one of the research questions. Appendix

B provides a graphic representation of the data collection method and associated component of the case study.

Trustworthiness

Creswell (2014) noted case studies are a qualitative design of inquiry in which the researcher develops and in-depth analysis of a program, event, organization, or process. The researcher utilized three methods of data collection: podcasts, document analysis, and an open-ended email survey to examine the organizational culture at the subject company. This triangulation of data provided three different sources of information from three areas of the company: founders and leaders, electronic communications via the company website, and surveys of employees not serving as founders or leaders at the time of the study.

Credibility

The design and implementation of a variety of data sources and participants within various levels of the organizational structure enhanced overall study quality, credibility, and trustworthiness (Baxter & Jack, 2008). The foundation of clearly written research questions, purposeful strategies, systematically managed data collection, and proper analysis utilizing functions and features of Microsoft Office software and Qualtrics software promoted data credibility, or truth value, as noted by Baxter and Jack (2008).

Dependability and Confirmability

Qualitative research is a valued paradigm of inquiry and the complexity that surrounds qualitative research requires rigorous and methodical methods to create useful results (Nowell et al., 2017). The researcher utilized thematic analysis for podcast data and document analysis. Thematic analysis is a useful method for examining perspectives of participants, comparing data from a variety of participants, and generating unanticipated insights (Nowell et al., 2017). Using Schein's (2004) framework as a guide, coupled with analysis of viewpoints and information from employees at all levels of the company, the researcher administered a comprehensive analysis of organizational culture of a startup company.

Transferability

The researcher aimed to collect and analyze the information from this organizational culture study to transfer the knowledge to other businesses, teams, or groups seeking guidance on defining values, communication, and culture creation. This research study could serve as a guide for start-up companies seeking data to create their business culture, and established companies or organizations seeking data to redefine or change the dynamics of their organizational culture. Research by Tran (2017) detailed culture, leadership, and management of Google and Zappos, companies dedicated to fostering a positive organizational culture from the lens of Schein (2017). This research study could build on research of similar companies, organizational culture, and startups in a various of industries.

Triangulation

Triangulation consists of utilizing different data sources of information by examining evidence from the sources and using it to build a coherent justification for themes (Creswell, 2014). Validity of the study was established by collecting data from founders, leaders, and employees in non-leadership positions. Further, utilizing three forms of data collection including podcasts, document analysis and email surveys converged several sources of data and perspectives from participants for validity (Creswell, 2014).

Ethical Considerations

Approval to conduct this research was obtained from company founder and current Chief Executive Officer of the startup athletic apparel company. The leaders and founders agreed to allow the researcher to explore their company culture via podcast data, document analysis, and online survey methods. Podcast data online revealed employee names and gender. For this study, names were excluded from the findings. Job titles were assigned a participant number and utilized to reference department leaders in the study analysis. Table 2 provides the reader with a description and classification of podcast participants and their associated job title within the company. For transparency and ethics, all research results will be shared with the subject company leaders upon completion of analysis. The researcher will return analyzed data to the subject company. Triangulation of data through multiple data collection provided knowledge about the single phenomenon, organizational culture of a startup company (Birt et al., 2016).

Delimitations

This study incorporated podcast interview data, document analysis of the company website data, and an open-ended survey. The three sources of data included information collected from founders and leaders of the company, public documents with details of words, videos, and pictures to depict the company, and a survey of employees in non-leadership positions. The researcher's triangulation of data from different sources built a coherent justification for themes because employees at all levels of the company will be included as participants (Creswell, 2014).

Delimitations to this study include selection of specific podcasts from the founders. There were a multitude of podcasts available for review by the researcher. The researcher utilized podcasts directly associated with organizational culture within the company. Utilization of the entire podcast series produced by the company might have provided additional insight on culture, although not the subject of processes, strategies, related to the research questions. The document analysis was limited to website data related to the company culture including the mission statement, job postings at the time of the study, values, and organizational structures. The open-ended survey for employees in non-leadership positions was limited in scope to reflect questions related to Schein's (2004) culture framework and the organizational culture of the subject company. At the time of the study, 80 employees were categorized as serving in non-leadership positions and eligible for participation in the survey method. As the company grows, that number, and scope of data collection via survey could significantly expand the insight from employees.

Summary

This case study explored the defined artifacts, values, norms, and underlying assumptions of a startup athletic apparel company utilizing the framework of Schein's (2017) culture research. The researcher aimed to understand and explore the connection between the theoretical framework and elements of organizational culture within the subject company. The participants were the founders, leaders, and employees of an athletic apparel company located in Los Angeles, California. Data collection methods included podcast interview data, document analysis, and email surveys. The researcher gathered data from leaders, department heads, and employees in non-leadership positions to conduct a complete analysis of the organizational culture of the company. Podcast participants were not identified by name, only job title. Survey participants remained anonymous due to use of Qualtrics for survey administration. Data were coded and analyzed to seek themes and connections between values, areas of focus, communication practices, and overall organizational culture. Appendix B details each research question, the element of Schein's (1983) framework associated to analysis, and the instrument utilized to collect specific to each question. In Chapter Four, the researcher will discuss the findings of the data.

Chapter Four: Findings

Overview

The purpose of this study was to explore the organizational culture of a startup athletic apparel company. Utilizing Schein's (2004) model of organizational culture as the framework, the researcher explored the artifacts, norms, values, and underlying assumptions of the company related to creation and sustainability of the organization's culture. The impact of culture within an organization is a critical element in day-to-day business practices (Burkus, 2014). Performance metrics can go up and down, but the strength of culture can provide consistency for employees within an organization (Sinek, 2017). Cultures are like precious and prized treasures when they are strong, healthy, and driving the right behaviors. They are among the greatest assets an organization can have (Warrick, 2017). Therefore, the study of organizational culture is applicable to a variety of business and professional settings.

The participants of this study were employees of the athletic apparel company. The researcher utilized podcast interview data, document analysis, and surveys to examine principles and practices related to culture creation within the athletic apparel business. Data from a variety of sources provided the researcher with a comprehensive understanding of the operations, values, and overall focus on startup company culture within the subject organization. Each research question was aligned with a specific element of Schein's (2004) framework coupled with one or more data collection methods to obtain a comprehensive examination of the organizational culture of a startup athletic apparel company.

The results of the study determined Schein's (2004) framework was evident within the creation and sustainability of the startup company culture. Employees within each level of the company's organizational structure provided consistent evidence of artifacts, norms, values, and underlying assumptions unique to the subject company. The company founders initiated a focus on company culture from the beginning. As the company experienced growth, the founders continued to focus on culture. By creating and changing strategies and processes throughout the growth process, the mission and goals related to fostering a positive organizational culture are evident and consistent.

The podcast data from company founders and leaders provided information about thoughts, goals, and processes of focusing on creating a positive organizational culture from a startup perspective. Data from employee surveys were consistent with the goals, values, and strategies the leaders put in place to create a company with a sustainable organizational culture. Consistency between leader data and data collected from employees in non-leadership positions analyzed within Schein's (2004) framework examined the leaders' and founders' efforts to foster a positive organizational culture from the company's existence to present.

Research Questions

This case study examined the organizational structures and processes, strategies and goals, and sources of values and action in a startup athletic apparel company. Utilizing the organizational culture framework of Schein (2004), the researcher examined the artifacts, norms and values, and underlying assumptions of the subject company. Data collected from podcasts, document analysis, and surveys were analyzed using themes and elements of organizational culture. The case study was structured with research questions, Schein's (2004) framework, and instruments to provide a comprehensive qualitative analysis of the organizational culture of a startup company. The research questions were:

RQ1: What are the organizational structures and processes that contribute to the creation and sustainability of the organizational culture?

RQ2: What are the values, strategies, and goals that determine the organizational culture at a startup athletic apparel company?

RQ3: What are actions, perceptions, and beliefs within the culture that are mutually reinforced by leaders and employees?

Table 1

Organization of the Case Study Elements

Research Question	Element of Schein's Framework	Instrument
RQ1	Artifacts	Document Analysis Podcasts
RQ2	Values	Podcasts
RQ3	Assumptions	Employee Survey Podcasts

Results

An organization's culture manifests within different levels of the company's structure. Observed patterns of behavior that create an organization's culture are attributed to the company values, norms, and artifacts. Organizational norms derive from values and manifest in artifacts. Schein's (1992) research attests artifacts are the most visible layer of organizational culture with values and norms being less visible. A visual representation would be an iceberg. The artifacts are visible above the water's surface, and the norms, values, and assumptions are not visible to those outside of the organization. Employees, leaders, and founders are the catalysts for creation and sustainability of the norms, values, and assumptions. Cultures are vulnerable assets that can be damaged or lost if leaders and founders of organizations are not aware or attentive to the value of a strong culture (Warrick, 2017). Culture can overcome the seemingly invincible structural barriers of an era and transform the behavior of entire industries and social systems (Horowitz, 2019). Each of those elements of Schein's (1992) model impact the artifacts visible to external stakeholders. Each element of the framework provides evidence in the form of organizational symbols, rituals, language, and physical workplace arrangements.

Figure 3

Illustration of Schein's model of organizational culture

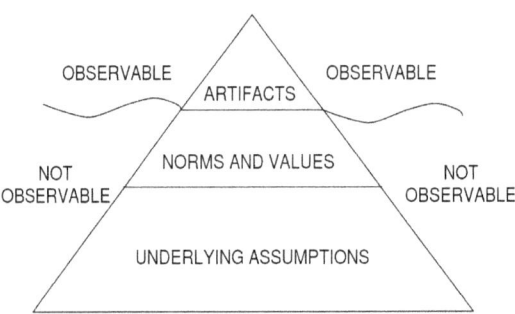

Note. This figure was obtained from Gerras et al. (2008).

Data Analysis and Themes

To examine elements of organizational culture in a case study format, the researcher transcribed 18 podcast interviews and created one document for all the podcast data. Utilizing color coding, the researcher used three different colors to highlight data in a Microsoft Word document separated into three categories of the iceberg: artifacts, norms and values, and assumptions Each of the three colors used for the three elements of Schein's (2004) framework were entered into separate documents. Next, the researcher coded each of the three documents separately and determined common themes within each framework element.

Utilizing the transcribed podcast data, the researcher repeated the data organization and did two rounds of coding using in vivo coding. The researcher examined elements of organizational culture unique to the subject company in which leaders of the company described artifacts, norms and values, and assumptions in their own words, unique to this company culture. Exploring the uniqueness of the company provided insight on education for group members, the employees. The cultural ideals present within organizations, coupled with communication and reinforcement are the foundation of building a strong culture (Warrick, 2017). Table 2 provides an outline of podcast interviewees, the department leaders, and the designated departmental leader structure at the time of the case study. Results and emergent themes from coding are presented in this chapter.

Table 2

Podcast Interviews with Company Leaders

Name	Department
Leader 1 (L1)	Chief Executive Officer/Founder
Leader 2 (L2)	Distribution Center Manager
Leader 3 (L3)	Customer Service Manager
Leader 4 (L4)	Direct to Consumer
Leader 5 (L5)	Operations
Leader 6 (L6)	Human Resources
Leader 7 (L7)	Activations
Leader 8 (L8)	Project Manager
Leader 9 (L9)	Sales
Leader 10 (L10)	Product
Leader 11 (L11)	Copy and Content
Leader 12 (L12)	Brand and Design
Leader 13 (L13)	Finance

Organizational Structures and Processes

RQ1 (What are the organizational structures and processes that contribute to the creation and sustainability of the organizational culture?) guided the examination of artifacts of the startup company's culture. Schein (2004) defined artifacts as all the phenomena one sees, hears, and feels when one encounters a new group with an unfamiliar culture. Data analysis of podcast interviews and analysis of documents provided evidence of visible organizational structures and processes within the startup company culture.

Two main themes emerged from analysis of the startup company's structures and processes: 1) communication, and 2) transparency. Brown's (2018) research determined a mantra of *Clear is Kind*. The startup company utilized Brene Brown's book *Dare to Lead* within their onboarding process as part of training and development related to culture. The company's structures and processes center around communication, sharing information, having difficult conversations when needed, and defining roles and objectives for every employee, every department, and company as a unit to solidify a foundation for a sustainable focus on organizational culture.

A focus on communication was evident in podcast interviews with leaders of the startup company. Podcast participant L1, the company Chief Executive Officer, described the communication within the company by stating,

> There is a huge transparency and accountability element of using Slack (a software that allows users to login and view information, converse, and collaborate). We have company-wide threads, basic announcements for all employees, and each product launch has its own thread. Within Slack, everyone is seeing information. So, people can't hide if you need information. You have the power to go and see. I think the transparency and accountability it has provided has been amazing.

Podcast participant L1 described communication and transparency as a broad, company-wide structure.

> Each flock (department) has values. They have slippery and supportive behaviors for their values. Slippery behaviors do not support values. Supportive behavior leans into values. Flocks have areas of focus related to their values. Each team member has a role that speaks to each of those elements. Teaching people that there are checkpoints with performance reviews focused on autonomy, mastery, and purpose, called AMP reviews.

Podcast participant L2 described communication processes by stating,

> My team gathers to discuss the number of orders in the system and look for red flags. We discuss daily roles of printing, picking, pack, box restock, and processing returns. Gold stars are handed out to people on the team, and we start the day. It is quick, but very grounding. We also have lunch together most days and some of our team has a weekly bike ride before work. Our warehouse and offices are in the same space, and it keeps departments connected.

Podcast participant L5 noted levels of transparency by stating, "nobody gets in trouble for making mistakes at this company, only for trying to hide them".

Podcast participant L9 described the lack of commission-based pay for the sales team in the context of communication and transparency.

> If you are really committed to the brand, you love the messaging. You love the feel, you love the culture. You're not going to just be focused on hitting a quota. You're going to be focused on always elevating the brand in all the different regions. Commission also puts a preface that the sales team is more important than other teams that they should get paid more or

a percentage of the company. Why would sales get that and not marketing or a distribution center? No commission allows everybody to know they are working together towards one. We just happen to be the cause of selling the product.

Artifacts related to clear communication channels included no internal email within the company; a comprehensive three-month onboarding process; onboarding as a cohort with team building and relationship building from the start; employees in the office two days per week (Tuesdays, and Thursdays), and an all staff meeting every Tuesday. With an entire podcast dedicated to discussing the company policy of no internal email, Participant L1 described the concept with research by stating,

> This is my favorite. The time savings according to *Forbes*, the average worker spends two and a half hours per day on email. If you reduce that by just 40%, which what I estimate we do, it saves over six work weeks per year per person. Six work weeks per year per person: the bandwidth, the autonomy, and the transparency this has created has been remarkable."

The concept further described by Participant L1:

> If information involving a project is something everybody needs to know about, with email, it is dumped into an inbox. You can't track it without the really awful way of catching upon an entire conversation by reading thread stacked upon thread. With Slack, when you want to work on a project, you can go to that project, and so it allows you to stay present and engaging things you want to engage in and not on others.

Artifacts related to transparency included a quarterly summit for all employees to celebrate successes and failures. Each employee reads specific books and participates in book club as a learning process related to organizational culture efforts and outcomes. Use of Slack (a software for sharing information and data) allows employees to upload information, exchange ideas, and do so in one place for everyone to see. Internal communications utilize Slack instead of email. The transparency element is every employee can see conversations, ask, and answer questions about specific projects, and leaders do not have to hold and disseminate information to every individual. The information, data, calendars, and planning work are done for everyone to access. Participant L1 describes the transparency element by stating,

> There's a hug transparency and accountability element of using Slack at our company. We have some company-wide threads, just basic announcements, project and team threads, and each product launch has its own Slack page. With any product launch, anyone at the company can go to the Slack page and see what's going on. I think the transparency and accountability it's provided has been quite amazing. Everyone has the power to go and see.

Pay scales are transparent, and company values are specifically defined with action-based deliverables associated with each value. The company values are fun and authenticity. The transparency related to those values is an aspect the company founders and leaders brought from Brown's (2018) research in the book club, and onboarding reading selection, *Dare to* Lead. Founders and leaders created lists of supporting behaviors, those behaviors that reinforce the values. And, in contrast, slippery behaviors are those behaviors that do not support the company values. Participant L1 described the rationale for implementing Brown's (2018) system of values creation and implementation by stating,

> We decided to make multiple supporting and slippery behaviors that speak to each of our values, so we know how to act, and we know when we're on track and when we're off track. For example, for the value of fun, one of the pillars is inclusion. Being inclusive is really fun. We are at our best when we are including everyone from our staff to our customers, everyone that we come in contact with. A supporting behavior for fun is using models that look like normal people. A slippery behavior is using typical fitness models.

Participant L1 further described the process and dedication to creating supporting and slippery behaviors for each value by noting, "at last count, we have over 60 examples of supporting for and values. And, we had a matching slippery behavior for each. We continually add on and share information with the team, and this has been hugely beneficial."

The artifacts of the startup company culture are centered around the people within the company. From clearly defined and communicated values, to full transparency on most business process, decisions, strategies, the startup athletic apparel company focused on people first. A notable quote by Participant L1 related to people and the leadership of a culture-focused company was evident in his statement,

> Treat people like adults and they'll act like adults. When you talk to people like adults, you realize how smart people are when you treat them

smart. Trust is built over time, and this is how we build trust in our culture
over time. It is a long game. I need to lead by example.

Data collected from 18 podcasts and document analysis were entered into a word cloud generator to examine most-used terms related to artifacts. The word cloud provided depicted organizational structures and processes are focused on people and their role(s) within the organization with the word *people* used most often in the data.

Company Values, Strategies, and Goals

RQ2 (What are the values, strategies, and goals that determine the organizational culture at a startup athletic apparel company?) was utilized to explore strategies, goals, philosophies, and adopted principles evident in the organizational culture. Schein (2004) attested beliefs, norms, and values require social validation by the group or organization members. As the group learns certain beliefs and values initially promulgated by the founder and leaders, they become norms. Data on the supported way of life, the beliefs, values, and norms, within a startup company was the focus of this question. Data analysis of podcast interviews provided the values, strategies, and goals related to organizational culture.

Emergent themes related to values, strategies, and goals were: 1) defined values, and; 2) creating connection between people, their jobs, and internal and external operations of the company. Company leaders utilized Brown's (2018) research noting defined values for organizations should not exceed two to three. The athletic apparel company took research-based evidence on value creation and strategized by creating two values for each department within the company. The values for each department are listed in Table 3.

Table 3

Defined Values for Each Department

Department	Values
Distribution Center	Teamwork; Responsibility
Customer Service	Teamwork; Consistency
Direct to Consumer	Innovation; Perseverance
Operations	Reliability; Learning
Human Resources	Integrity; Connection
Activations	Preparation; Connection
Project Management	Organization; Accountability
Sales	Risk-taking; Community
Product	Quality; Efficiency
Copy and Content	Creativity; Harmony
Brand and Design	Resiliency; Transparency
Finance	Financial Stability; Curiosity

Within the subject company, employees, processes, and goals are guided by the company values, fun and authenticity, and two additional values specific to their department. Clear, concise, achievable goals for each role, every employee, and each department, created a cohesive, transparent element of Schein's (2004) framework applied to this startup company. Department leader, podcast participant L7 stated, "our values are connection and preparation. We support those values with areas of focus including expertise, cohesion, and hype. The department is responsible for organic social posting, interacting with followers, and creating energy (giveaways)." Another departmental leader, podcast participant L13 noted,

> Our flock values are financial stability and curiosity. Those values go hand in hand with foresight. All the actions of each flock impact our bottom line. If we see a red flag, we need to be comfortable speaking up and looking to the future to see how today's decisions impact tomorrow.

A company founder, participant L1, stated, "decisions are made at all levels of the organization by applying the values, fun and authenticity. If a business decision does not align with the values, it does not move forward." The founder referenced terminology used by Brown (2018), areas of focus and supporting and slippery behaviors, as a focus on success or falling behind. The company founder stated, "values and areas of focus are supported by clearly defined supporting behaviors, those aligned with goals, and slippery behaviors, those not aligned with achieving goals. The employee's role is their boss."

Podcast participant L10 described the foundational norms of the product team by stating,

> I first heard of the four Fs in my initial conversations with the company founder when we were talking about me coming on board at the company. The four Fs are not about one person or two people's opinions. There is a lens with which anybody can evaluate product. It spoke volumes and it meant that anybody could be a contributor as long as they were answering those questions related to our values and the foundation of the four Fs: fun, fashion, function, and (af)fordable.

Evidence of norms included clearly defined job descriptions so every employee in the company knows their role and the role of others. Another norm was autonomy. Podcast participant L1 stated, "employees choose how they do their job, when they do their job, but not what they do." With a liberal hybrid work model, two days in the office per week, Tuesdays and Thursdays, employees have the freedom to choose how and when they work, but must show work is being done, progress being made, and goals being met.

The data collected related to norms, values, and beliefs aligns with data collected in RQ1 in that people are the focus of this element of organizational culture. The people-focused approach to culture was evident in podcast participant L6's quote, "employees are provided tools, support, and feedback to do their best work." Participant L6 also noted, "Personal improvement plans are used if employees are not meeting expectations. This effort is to serve the person and their role in the company." The company founder stated, "We want members of our flock (employees) to keep grounded, be involved in the community, and participate in community projects. We create purpose by empowering employees to volunteer to keep grounded and choose projects related to their happiness and interests."

Data collected from podcasts were entered into a word cloud generator to examine most-used words within the data. The most used word in the data from organizational values, strategies, and goals in a startup company was *people*. The word counts also determined a focus on values, time, and fun.

Actions, Perceptions, and Beliefs Within the Company

RQ3 (What are the actions, perceptions, and beliefs within the culture that are mutually reinforced by leaders and employees?) was utilized to examine the underlying assumptions within the startup company culture. Schein's (2004) framework visually depicts cultural elements deemed underlying assumptions as actions, perceptions, and beliefs "beneath the surface". Those actions, perceptions, and beliefs are elements of organizational culture mutually reinforced by leaders and employees. Schein (2004) attested assumptions are an organization's ultimate sources of values and actions as this level of culture encompasses unconscious, taken-for-granted, thoughts and feelings. Podcasts and surveys administered to company employees not serving in leadership positions provided elements of culture categorized as underlying assumptions.

Data analysis of podcast interviews demonstrated themes of: 1) fun; 2) creativity; and; 3) cohesion as thoughts and feelings of department leaders at the subject company. Themes were evident in the tone of interviewee interactions with the interviewer. Participant L1 stated, "we are all about "F" words: Fun, Fashion, and Function!" Each department leader detailed their "lame title and real title" as a play on words related to their job functions. Participant L3 stated, "my department's lame title is Customer Service Team. Our real title is Squawk and Awe." Participant L8 stated, "my department's lame title is Project Managers. Our real title is Puppet Masters." Participant L11, which is also a co-founder of the startup, stated, "my lame title is Head of Content and Copy. At this company, my title is Chief Dreams Orchestrator because our content team is called the Department of Dreams."

The company created a mascot, Carl the Flamingo. Flamingo references are made throughout documents, website data, and both internal and external communications. Weekly meetings are specifically called "Tuesdays with Carl". Departments are called "flocks" and department leaders are called "flock leaders". The department names use of the word flock and flamingo references and themes in all company communications indicate a team/family approach to business with an element of fun, one of the company values. Podcast participant L1 shared, "if an employee gets a tattoo of Carl the Flamingo, they can expense it." Participant L13 noted, "catered lunches for the office and monthly allowances for team connection is centered around fun. Expensing Uber and Lyft rides for company events is also something we find necessary that other companies definitely do not do." Participant L1 added, "you get 70 pairs of sunglasses a year. That is fun."

In relation to data collected for RQ1 and RQ2, the books utilized for onboarding and book club learning processes produced slogans and internal communications evident in underlying assumptions at the startup company. Terminology such as, "Done is better than perfect", "Clear is Kind" (Brown, 2018), and "Getting Things Done" (GTD) from David Allen's book *Getting Things Done* are evident in founder and leader podcast interviews. Data shows there is a cohesive and consistent communication within the company from artifacts, norms and values, and underlying assumptions. Participant L6 stated,

> During our onboarding process we're shifting people's paradigm into the thought of everything is possible here. But you must own it. You have autonomy and you live into these things and the realization that everything is possible. It is a yes culture, not a no culture where people are stuck in their ways. The biggest shift

underneath everything we do is shifting the paradigm to communicate to employees that it's all possible.

In each podcast interview with departmental leaders, the company founder, Participant L1, asks them to discuss their spirit animal. The tone of voice, significant and consistent laughter associated with spirit animal discussions, and creativity displayed by leaders provided evidence of the company values, fun and authenticity. It was a fun method for learning more about leaders as individuals. Each leader had the opportunity to detail why they associated themselves with a specific animal. Their choices depicted values important to them as individuals. Participant L4 described the spirit animal choice as,

> My spirit animal is a kraken. I like the symbolism of the giant sea monster being able to crush ships at sea and when you cut its arms, they grow back stronger. Participant L12 stated, "my spirit animal is a red panda, honestly, for no major reason. At the time, I was really into the that they were cute, and they were hilarious online. Not sure what that says about me, but I just identify with it and love it.

The leader of the finance team, participant L13, described her spirit animal as, "a lion because they're beautifully intimidating and protective".

Department, or flock, leaders were asked about their biggest mistake. The verbiage used in the interview was an "f-word" which correlates with previous data related to the company founder's comment, "we focus on F-words, fun, function, and fashion". One leader noted, "owning mistakes is encouraged and practiced by leaders. Awards are given for the biggest mistake each quarter." The focus on celebrating and acknowledging mistakes for learning purposes was an underlying assumption noted by several departmental leaders in their podcast interviews.

Data examined for underlying assumptions at the startup company depict a consistency, from onboarding throughout employment, with a focus on values and an understanding that organizational culture is a process, not a product. Company leaders put people first, and noted by the founder, "leaders recognize need for transparency and change processes. As a startup company, understanding and embracing change is valued by leaders." The human resources team internally deemed the "ministry of culture", is tasked with making sure everyone is having fun through individual growth and creating connections. The human resources leader described stage one of the hiring process included a requirement for job applicants to draw a picture of a pirate fighting an octopus. The human resources leader, participant L6, stated,

> This is just brilliant, and it wasn't my idea. It is a great filter to make sure people are reading the entire job posting and following directions. If they are not willing to do it for whatever reason, it's silly, it's dumb, whatever they are saying to themselves, they will not fit into the culture at this company.

In the research, evidence emerged in detailed actions related to jobs, roles, and leadership initiatives directed within each individual department and consistent across all departments. Data collected from podcasts were entered into a word cloud generator to determine most-used words within the data. People, the most-used word in the underlying assumptions data, mirrors the results of word cloud data from artifacts, norms, and values.

Additional data was collected and analyzed for research RQ3 from employee surveys. Employees in non-leadership positions at the subject company provided organizational culture insight from the company's internal operations. At the time of the study, the employee survey was made available to approximately 80 employees in non-leadership positions at the startup company. A response rate of 50% was achieved. Leading journals recognize an appropriate response rate of 30 to 40% and attribute publishing articles with response rates at or greater than that range (Story & Tait, 2019).

The survey was administered online and was accessible to the participants for a 15-day period. Participants were asked to report the length of time they had been employed at this company, their age, gender, level of education, and current employment status. Each of these survey components were multiple choice questions. Demographical survey results are included in Tables 4 through 8.

Table 4

Length of Employment at Startup Company

Length of Employment	%	Count
Less than one year	47.5	19
1 year to 2 years	15	6
2 years to 4 years	37.5	15
4 years to 6 years	0	0
6 years or more	0	0

Note. n=40

Most employees surveyed had been employed at the company for less than one year and no more than four years. This startup company was seven years old at the time of the case study. Therefore, this data is indicative to the growth of the company expanding at a rapid pace. The next demographic figure represents the age of survey participants. Table 5 provides data on age ranges of employees in non-leadership positions at the startup company.

Table 5

Participant Age

Age	%	Count
18-29 years old	40	16
30-30 years old	42.5	17
40-49 years old	15	6
50-59 years old	2.5	1
60 or older	0	0

Note. n=40

A significant percentage of employees were 39 years of age and younger. A total of 17 participants, making of the highest count of age ranges, were 30-39 years of age. Survey participants in the 18–29-year-old range made up 40% of the sample for a total of 16 employees. The third demographical statistic from the survey sought to collect information about the gender of participants. The survey asked participants to describe their gender as male, female, or other. Table 6 provides data on gender of survey participants.

Table 6

Participant Gender

Gender	Number of Employees	Percentage of Survey Respondents
Male	10	25%
Female	30	75%
Other	0	0%

Note. n=40

The fourth demographic data collection in the survey requested participants indicate their highest level of education. Table 7 provides a detailed outline of levels of education of employees in non-leadership positions at the startup company.

Table 7

Level of Education

Education Level	%	Count
Less than a high school diploma	0	0
High school degree or equivalent	0	0
Some college, no degree	2.5	1
Associate Degree	2.5	1
Bachelor's Degree	75	30
Master's Degree	20	8
Doctorate or Professional Degree	0	0

Note. n=40

Data collected from the survey to determine current employment status of survey respondents indicated that 100% of the 40 employees surveyed were employed full time, which was classified as 40 hours or more per week. A graphical representation of employment status is depicted in Table 8.

Table 8

Current Employment Status

Employment Category	%	Number of employees
Employed full time (>40 hrs/wk)	100%	40
Employed part time (<39 hrs/wk)	0%	0

Note. n=40

The first part of the survey aimed to collect data about employee demographics. The second part of the survey utilized open-ended survey questions to explore topics in depth, to understand processes, and to identify potential causes of observed correlations (Weller et al., 2018). The researcher utilized open-ended questions to seek perspectives on organizational culture at a startup company from the employees serving in non-leadership positions. As previously stated, a 50% response rate was achieved. The employee survey focused on seeking insight on RQ3, "what are actions, perceptions, and beliefs within the culture that are mutually reinforced by leaders and employees?" Schein's (2004) organizational culture framework focus of underlying assumptions, described by the author as actions, assumptions, and beliefs "beneath the surface", was the element of the theoretical framework examined.

The first open-ended question asked participants to describe a scenario where the company core value of "fun" was exemplified in a work setting. Responses solicited from participants relating the value of fun included quarterly meets/summit with all employees; Tuesday company-wide meetings; company outings such as bowling and happy hour; and games played during the onboarding process including a company-wide scavenger hunt. One participant stated, "discussing what we do outside of work so we can relate and share good stories." Another survey respondent noted, "adding fun details to otherwise monotonous tasks", while a third person stated, "fun is amplified every day!" Another perspective from the survey found work-focused fun such as, "being prepared and showing up with great ideas" and "coming up with fun and playful responses to reply to our customers through email." In summary, the words "every day" and "fun" were used throughout responses to this question such as "every day there is some element of fun."

The second open-ended question seeking to examine underlying assumptions asked participants to describe a word or phrase that comes to mind when employees think of the leaders of the startup company. Overall, the responses were positive, and some responses were repeated by more than one participant. Similar words and phrases were combined by the researcher and a list of leadership description data is in Table 9.

Table 9

Employee Descriptions of Company Leaders: Positive and Negative Descriptions

Positive Responses	Negative Responses
Visionaries	Self-serving
Collaborative	Uncompassionate
Inspiring	Toxic Positivity
Better than most	Green
Multi-faceted and understanding	Energetic and brilliant, but disorganized
Forward Thinking	Separate
Culture setters	
Quirky	
Hardworking	
Passionate	
Funny	
Respectful	
Open-minded	
Genuinely care for employees	
Willing to sit down and spend time with anyone	
Supportive	
Authentic	
Innovative	

In analyzing the data from this question and responses listed above, employees are more than three times as likely to associate a positive word or phrase to describe leaders than a partially negative, or negative word or phrase to describe leaders of the startup company. There were 18 positive responses and six negative responses to this question. Data collected from this survey question was entered into a word cloud generator to determine most-used words by employees. The word most used to describe leaders was "supportive" followed by "driven", "inspire", "passionate", and "authentic", a company core value.

The third open-ended survey question asked participants about a time when the participant failed, and how company leaders responded to that failure. Many responses produced themes of support, understanding, respect, fairness, and an openness to owning failures. Participants used words such as, "respect", "fair", "learning experience", "support and conversation", "honesty", and "growth opportunity". Previous data from podcasts provided details about the company giving an award for the biggest mistake at each quarterly summit. Survey participants provided consistent information related to owning failures, having a sense of humor, and constructive feedback for learning. A total of 15% of participants responded that they had yet to experience failure due to being newly hired, or not working for the company long enough to have had this experience.

The fourth open-ended survey question asked participants to describe a scenario when leaders or fellow employees led by example. 20% of participants described a scenario in which the Chief Executive Officer led by example. Those responses included,

- "Our CEO shares his own failures and proposes solutions openly."
- "Our CEO gives his performance review on stage in front of the entire company."
- "Our CEO gives clear, objective feedback during every meeting."
- "Our CEO encourages personal time off."
- "CEO leads work sessions to help organize when departments are overwhelmed."

Survey participants described a scenario in which their department leader exemplified leading by example. A total of 17.5% of responses included a reference to a departmental leader. Those responses included:

- "My flock leader routinely demonstrates saying "no". She works incredibly hard and can sometimes take on too much. When her plate is full, I have seen her say "no". This awareness is celebrated and supported by her supervisor."
- "Flock leader diving into details and getting dirty with the rest of the team when needed."
- "Encourages team to be thought leaders and consistently looks for their opinion and back it when it is questioned in meetings."
- "A leader exercised patience in getting me the answer that I needed."
- "A leader at our company owned a mistake, apologized to the person, and discussed the mistake at an all-staff meeting."
- "When leaders initiate something, they expect of other leaders in the company, it reinforces that showing up from the top-down matters."

Other themes that emerged from the question of leading by example included: teamwork, transparency, quality of work, specifically presentations, and prepared and organized leaders.

Lastly, 5% of responses detailed scenarios in which the participant felt others did not lead by example. An additional 5% did not respond to the survey question. Participant responses in this category included:

- "I don't see this a lot unfortunately."
- "I have not seen a scenario like this currently in the company."

Employees in non-leadership positions at the startup company provided detailed survey responses, both positive and negative, in describing scenarios of leading by example. Of the 40 survey participants, 90% of the responses were positive and 5% of responses were negative, and 5% did not respond to the question.

The last open-ended question in the employee survey asked participants about the one aspect they would change to improve the organizational culture at the startup company. Five themes emerged from this survey question with the results presented in Table 10.

Table 10

Employee Suggestions for Changes Related to Culture

Percentage of responses	Theme
25%	No changes: "Nothing"
12.5%	Workplace structure changes: "More flexible hours" "Choice of in-office workdays" "Less meetings" "Get rid of purpose and mastery projects due to workload"
12.5%	Managing growth: "Promote from within" "Manage growth" "Startup pains are evident, but do not impact culture."
10%	People-focused changes: "Inclusion for introverts" "Some activities are overwhelming for introverts" "Expand what inclusion means at the company" "Make quarterly parties optional" "Better understand employees lives outside of work (Commute time)"

Table 10. (continued).

| 7.5% | Physical workspace:
"More space"
"Water slide in the office"
"There is a clear separation between the office and the distribution center – could benefit from the same purpose projects" |

The open-ended survey questions provided the researcher with a broad perspective of employee thoughts on aspects of underlying assumptions within the organizational culture of the startup company. Additionally, other elements of Schein's (2004) framework were evident in each survey question. Table 11 details each survey question and the framework elements present for data collection and analysis.

Table 11

Open-Ended Survey Questions and Schein's Framework Element

Survey Question	Schein's Organizational Culture Framework
SQ1: Describe "fun"	Assumptions/Values
SQ2: Describe company leaders	Assumptions
SQ 3: Describe a time you failed	Assumptions/Artifacts
SQ4: Describe "lead by example"	Assumptions/Norms and Values
SQ5: Describe one culture change	Assumptions/Norms and Values/Artifacts

Summary

The researcher aimed to examine the organizational culture of a startup company using podcast interview data, document analysis, and employee survey data to enhance the understanding of creating and sustaining organizational culture in this business setting. Each element of the case study provided data to support the company founders' people-first focus. Figures 5, 6, and 7 depict the people-first focus with graphical representation of most used words in the data related to artifacts, norms and values, and underlying assumptions (Schein, 2004). The word "people" was most used in each of the three categories of data collected from three different groups within the company, the founder, the departmental leaders, and employees. The consistency can be attributed to the company value of authenticity.

The elements of defined values, clear communication, and transparency were evident in the podcast interview data, document analysis, and employee surveys. Leaders and employees in non-leadership positions at the startup company provided consistent answers to questions about processes, structures, goals, actions, and the overall focus on people within the company. The graphic on the left side of Figure 9 from Gerras et al. (2008) depicts a visual representation of Schein's (2004) model of organizational culture, the theoretical framework of this study. The graphic on the right side of Figure 5, created by the author, contains the same elements of Schein's (2004) model in a different order.

Figure 5

A Comparison of Schein's Framework to Startup Company Framework

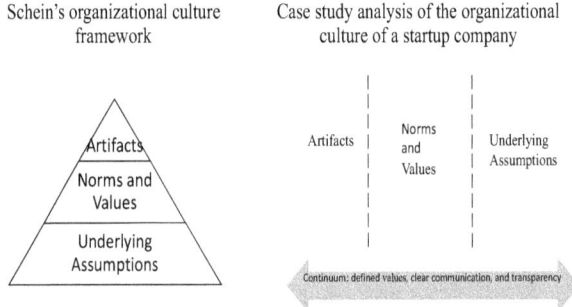

Podcast participant L6 specifically stated, "everything we do is shifting the paradigm. We deprogram new hires from traditional corporate culture and reprogram them to adapt to our culture." Those words coupled data collected within this study provide a sound summary of organizational culture creation and sustainability at a startup athletic apparel company. In Chapter five, the researcher will discuss how an athletic apparel startup company culture model could be utilized in a variety of business settings.

Chapter 5: Discussion and Conclusion

Overview

The purpose of this study was to explore how artifacts, norms and values, and underlying assumptions create and reinforce the organizational culture of a startup athletic apparel company based in California. By conducting a case study about this company, the researcher intended to explore how practices and norms within the organization's culture were influenced by the efforts of the founders and leaders. This chapter will provide insight by relating the findings to the literature review and the research questions. Schein's (2004) organizational culture framework, the theoretical foundation of the study, are compared to the research questions and findings. The researcher also addresses implications, limitations, and suggestions for future research.

Summary of Findings

The goal of this research study was to explore the organizational culture of a startup athletic apparel company. Startups are characterized by innovation, creativity, and rapid growth (Baldridge & Curry 2022). The case study examined how defined values, norms, and strategies created and reinforced the organizational culture of the subject company. Schein's (2004) organizational culture framework was the theoretical foundation of this study. Schein's (1983) culture research determined an organizational culture depends on a definable organization, in the sense of several people interacting with each other for the purpose of accomplishing some goal in their environment.

The use of multiple data sources provided triangulation of data collected from pre-recorded podcast interviews, document analysis of website information, and employee surveys. Data were used to explore and examine the artifacts, norms, values, and underlying assumptions of the organization's culture (Schein, 2004). Exploration of perspectives from company founders and leaders, public information on the company website, and employee perspectives provided a thorough review of the organization's culture.

Exploring the creation and sustainability of an organization's culture is a shared group phenomenon. Culture does not exist within a single person or within individual characteristics. It resides in shared behaviors, values, and assumptions experienced through norms and expectations of a group. Organizational culture is pervasive, enduring, and implicit. The creation and manifestation of a culture is influenced by collective behaviors, physical environments, visible symbols, and stories. The unseen aspects of culture development include mindsets, motivations, and unspoken assumptions (Groysberg et al., 2018). The concept of company leaders being a coach, as opposed to a critic has proven impactful on organizational culture (Bryant, 2011). Therefore, aspects of culture development coupled with the leadership of the organization are the pillars of a foundation for an organization's culture. A focus from leaders with the perspective that actual behaviors impacting the organization can be taught, measured, and evaluated. Culture creation and sustainability acts, not just aspires (Brown, 2012).

The study aimed to answer three research questions:

RQ1: What are the organizational structures and processes that contribute to the creation and sustainability of the organizational culture?

RQ2: What are the values, strategies, and goals that determine the organizational culture at a startup athletic apparel company?

RQ3: What are actions, perceptions, and beliefs within the culture that are mutually reinforced by leaders and employees?

Artifacts

RQ1 was utilized to explore artifacts related to the organizational culture of the subject company. Schein (2004) defined artifacts as all the phenomena one sees, hears, and feels when one encounters a new group with an unfamiliar culture. Data analysis of podcast interviews and analysis of documents, specifically website information, provided evidence of visible organizational structures and processes within the startup company culture.

Two themes emerged from analysis of the startup company's structures and processes: communication and transparency. Brown's (2018) research determined a mantra of *Clear is Kind*. The startup company utilized Brown's book *Dare to Lead* within their onboarding process as part of training and development related to culture. The company's structures and processes center around communication, sharing information, having difficult conversations when needed, and defining roles and objectives for every employee, department, and company as a unit to solidify a foundation for a sustainable focus on organizational culture. Understanding, evaluating, and focusing on communication as a culture analysis tool, provides great potential for leaders to solve practical challenges inside organizations. Sharing understandings helps employees successfully coordinate with one another. From onboarding to everyday interactions, personally and electronically, leaders can reinforce communication standards and methods to impact organizational culture (Corritore et al., 2020). Study participant L1 noted the value of authenticity related to structures and processes and themes of communication and transparency by stating, "we approach communication and actions with the perspective of if the goal is being authentic and people don't like you it's okay. If the goal is being liked and people don't like you, you're f*#@%." L1 discussed processes and strategies with the statement,

> We adapt and evolve quickly. We test things and if they work out great, and if they don't, we kill it and move on. Our ability to always be trying what's new and what's out there, and not hide behind the perfection is really important.

The approach from company founders and leaders is leadership and culture building takes practice. There is a universal understanding within the company that it is acceptable to pivot if change is needed. With the communication and transparency evident within the processes and strategies, organizational change, growth, and success is evident for the startup company.

    Data collected related to artifacts was evident with consistency between information shared by leaders in podcasts and information on the company website including the mission statement, job postings, and defined values. Dimensions applicable to the study of organizational culture regardless of type, size, industry, or geography are people interactions and response to change (Groysberg et al., 2018). The structures and processes driven by leadership that contribute to the creation and sustainability of the startup company's culture are strategic, consistent, and people-centered with communication and transparency as the path to growth and success. The subject company leaders approach leading as a practice and the mindset that if you want leaders, you must cultivate leaders. And, within processes and strategies, "the goal isn't to win every day.

The goal is to try", as stated by study participant L1. In summary, people report to managers, but they follow leaders (Bryant, 2011). This case study determined company leadership is valuable to the organizational culture artifacts.

Norms and Values

RQ2 focused on examining the values, strategies, and goals that determine the culture of the subject company. Schein (2004) attested beliefs, norms, and values require social validation by the group or organization members. As the group learns certain beliefs and values initially promulgated by the founder and leaders, they become norms. An introductory basis for understanding organizational cultures is *The Golden Rule* as defined by Greer and Shuck (2020). The authors define the *Rule* to challenge leaders to notice others, respond with dignity, be present in the moment, and live into real joy for the successes of others. Leaders modeling these practices showcase the importance of *The Golden Rule's* values and actions.

Leaders' actions significantly impact the present and future culture and organizational health within a company (Lencioni, 2012). Optimal performance by a team or organization is related to its history, strategy, resources, and competitiveness. But, more importantly, assessment of culture is directly related to values, beliefs, and behaviors of its members. Assessment of culture across a range of individuals in different roles and levels is essential to understanding the impact of organizational culture on teams, programs, units, and organizations (Cruickshank & Collins, 2012). This case study was designed to collect information from employees at all structural levels of the company. Company founders, departmental leaders, and employees in non-leadership positions provided insight on the culture to encompass a comprehensive view of the startup company's culture.

Beyond the research of Brown (2012) related to value implementation within an organization, the literature review provided insight on values and norms evident in a study of the automotive industry. The study determined aspects of a thriving culture were significantly influenced by leader behaviors centered around openness, motivation, and values. The outcomes of leader actions were a culture of creativity and innovation (Auernhammer & Hall, 2014). The versatility and transferability of study of this kind is applicable to many industries evident in the athletic apparel space to the automotive industry space. Data analysis of podcast interviews with company leaders provided the values, strategies, and goals related to the company's organizational culture.

Emergent themes related to values, strategies, and goals were: 1) defined values and 2) creating connection between people, their jobs, and internal and external operations of the company. Company leaders utilized Brown's (2018) research noting defined values for organizations should not exceed two to three. The subject company used research-based evidence on value creation and strategized by creating two values for each department within the company. The goal is that employees, processes, and goals are guided by the company values, fun and authenticity, and two additional values specific to their department. The startup athletic apparel company's values are not simply words listed on a poster in the office. With clarity guiding efforts, the company created two values, fun and authenticity for the entire organization. At the time of the case study, Participant L1, the company CEO, stated, "over 60 supporting and slippery behaviors have been determined for each value." Company leaders defined supporting behaviors as "those actions that speak to the values, so we know how to act, and we know when we're on track and when we're off track." In contract, a slippery behavior is an action not supporting the values. Each of the 12 departments within the company had two unique values specific to their function and duties. An example from study participant L2, "our flock (departmental) values are teamwork and responsibility. One person can only pack so many boxes a day and we want our customers to get the orders as they expected." Clear, concise, achievable goals for each role, every employee, and each department, created a cohesive, transparent element of Schein's (2004) framework applied to this startup company.

Data collected produced findings related to strategies and goals that mirrored the focus of the previous research question, people. Values and subsequent supporting and non-supporting behaviors were created with guidance from Brown's (2012) *Dare to Lead,* to help the people within the organization and define who and what the organization seeks to accomplish to external stakeholders. Strategies and goals within the subject company are people-centered and clearly designed and communicated with individual and team success as the goal for growth of the company.

Underlying Assumptions

RQ3 was utilized to examine the company's underlying assumptions of organizational culture. Schein (2004) attested assumptions are an organization's ultimate sources of values and actions as this level of culture encompasses unconscious, taken-for-granted, thoughts and feelings. Lencioni's (2012) research on leaders and organizations determined the organizational health of businesses and team units within a business. A healthy organization was defined as one with minimal politics, minimal confusion, and high morale. The impact on human capital provides a competitive advantage for the company. To assess the underlying assumptions of the subject company, the researcher used podcast interviews with company leaders. Additionally, employee surveys were administered to company employees not serving in leadership positions to provide elements of culture categorized as underlying assumptions.

The emergent themes and findings related to assumptions included consistency and communication. The researcher compared podcast data from the perspective of company leaders to data collected from employees in non-leadership positions. With a 50% survey response rate from employees, the data produced consistent underlying assumptions within the organization. Communication processes, both verbal and written, were consistent throughout the company. The understanding that leadership and organizational culture intersect in the arena of human influence is notable and applicable within the assumptions of an organization. There are two ways to influence human behavior: manipulate it or inspire it (Sinek, 2009). This case study determined the consistency between leader efforts related to organizational culture, and the impact those efforts have on the employees is profound. Their efforts categorized within the underlying assumptions element of the culture framework has proven they can rally employees not for a single event, but for years (Sinek, 2009). The findings examined actions, perceptions, and beliefs and found they are mutually reinforced by leaders and employees of the startup company. Their testament of why their organization exists is credited with leader understanding, clarifying, and living that why as a model behavior for the rest of the people within the organization (Sinek, 2009).

In summary, findings from the study determined artifacts, norms, values, and underlying assumptions are evident with the organizational culture of the subject company. Data collected in this study supports Schein's (2004) organizational culture framework. However, the study concludes the structure of the framework changes within the culture of a startup company. The traditional culture framework has a hierarchy of visible structures, deemed artifacts, and processes with norms, values, and assumptions, not visible to those outside of the organization. In contrast, data collected in this study from the startup company, depict a culture structure where structures, processes, norms, values, and assumptions are visible to everyone. The themes of organizational culture at a startup company include *transparency, communication, teamwork. support, respect,* and *growth.* The findings reinforce the people-focused mindset within the company's artifacts, norms, values, and assumptions. In contrast to previous research by Schein (2004), the study determined those elements of organizational culture framework are not a hierarchy. The elements are a continuum with fluid motion from artifacts to assumptions driven by communication, consistency, and transparency. The creation and sustainability of the organizational culture is a mutually reinforced process between leaders and employees. Figure 6 is a visual representation of the comparison between organizational culture frameworks. The graphic on the left from Gerras et al. (2008) is Schein's (2004) organizational culture framework. The graphic on the right was created by the researcher and adapted from Schein's (2004) model to provide the reader with a visualization of the organizational culture framework of a startup athletic apparel company.

Figure 6

A Comparison of Schein's Framework to Startup Company Framework

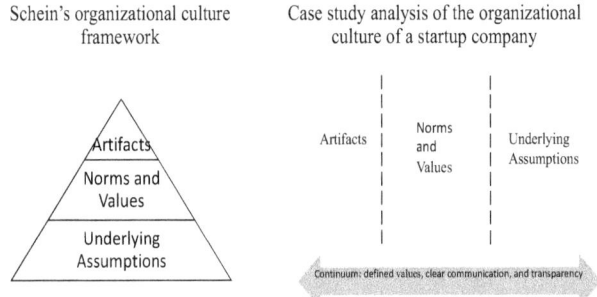

Discussion

The results of this study determined Schein's (2004) model of organizational culture depicted by the "iceberg" graphic, is still relevant in today's research on culture. These findings of this study reinforced the elements of the theoretical framework; artifacts, norms and values, and underlying assumptions, but with new, innovative pathways to creating and sustaining a positive organizational culture. Early research on organizational culture determined culture building was an element of leadership deemed as important and tactical as strategic thinking within organizations (Bass & Avolio, 1993). Beyond leadership, recent research culture determined when impactful elements of organizational culture are aligned, it can create energy towards a shared purpose. The result of a shared purpose throughout an organization is the capacity to thrive (Groysberg et al., 2018).

This study was not aimed at studying organizational culture during a worldwide pandemic. However, due to timing, the study was conducted during pandemic times. Despite the challenges posed by the pandemic and mandated safety measures, the findings determined the startup athletic apparel company maintained and sustained the culture initiatives and foundations despite external challenges. Some company structures in place prior to the pandemic proved to be of value during a transition to work away from the office. Study participant L1 stated, "our culture prides itself on raising adults. Our work from home policy calls for three days at home and two mandatory office days each week. We were uniquely qualified to thrive in a shelter-in-place scenario such as a pandemic. We were already video chat pros and we use Slack to communicate efficiently and effectively." The strength of the company values, clear communication channels, and a level of transparency between leaders and employees were artifacts, values, and assumptions allowed company founders and leaders to navigate challenging times. Additionally, many of their processes, strategies, and communication channels did not need to change because of the pandemic. Those challenging times, coupled with exponential growth as a startup, make this case study relevant, practical, and potential useful to be replicated by other businesses seeking to create or change their organizational culture.

Today's business landscape is ever-changing especially with a post pandemic world emerging with new perspectives on what work and a workplace look like. The subject company, as a startup, dedicated time, money, and focus on elements of the organizational culture from the beginning. Because workplace structures have changed and employees want more flexibility, more work-life balance, and a liberal work from home policy, company leaders are challenged to adjust traditional organizational culture structures and adhere to new ideas, policies, and strategies to run a successful business, but also have a renewed focus on the people, the employees, within the business.

As a teaching tool, the methods utilized to create the culture and adjust cultural elements with the growth of the company, could be of value to other businesses seeking to better define and streamline their organizational culture initiatives. Beyond startup companies, organizations with traditional structures, or no organizational culture structures, could utilize this study to implement and create a system to cultivate or reinvent archaic ways to institute a positive organizational culture. This study provides insight on creating values for a company and creatin values specifically for departments. From Brown's (2012) research supporting a very short list, two to three values, coupled with the practical implementation evident within the subject startup company, this information could be utilized by companies, business, departments, and teams, both large and small.

Implications

The results of this study provided theoretical, empirical, and practical implications. The theoretical implications indicated Schein's (2004) model of organizational culture including the elements, artifacts, norms, values, and underlying assumptions were evident in the results of the case study. However, while the elements of Schein's (2004) model are relevant in the creation and sustainability of the culture within a startup company, the hierarchy of how those elements interact, or impact one another in a business setting are slightly different in a startup company.

The empirical implications of this case study were evident in the lived experiences of the founders and leaders as determined by podcast data interviews. The company leaders chose to focus on creating and sustaining an organizational culture from the beginning. Their efforts to communicate, be transparent, and make changes as the company experienced growth were tied to their focus on organizational culture.

The practical implications of this study include its relevance to startup companies, and existing companies seeking to improve organizational culture. Many facets of business could benefit from the insight produced within this case study. Large companies, departments, teams, small businesses, and other groups or teams within those entities could utilize the information from this case study to plan for their organization related to creating and sustaining organizational culture. In addition, with a worldwide pandemic still requiring individuals and business to make adjustments, change goals, and create new strategies for growth, this information could be utilized to re-emerge from the pandemic with a new business plan and a focus on improving organizational culture.

Limitations

The limitations of this study included the worldwide pandemic and the rapid growth experienced by a startup company. These factors had the potential to impact data collected due to the timing of the study. The pandemic required businesses to adjust to a fully remote status. The rate of growth of a startup company had the potential for data, interview information, and perspectives to change over the course of the case study timeframe.

The subject company, located in California, had to conform to local and state regulations related to safety measures during the pandemic. The survey response rate for data collection was 50%, but answers related to organizational culture might have been somewhat different outside of the timing of the pandemic and its impact on personal and professional lives of employees due to businesses transitioning to work-from-home policies for safety measures.

Another limitation was the use of podcast data related to a startup company. Because the company was experiencing rapid growth as a startup, podcast data, while relevant and up to date at the time of recording and publication, could have experienced changing perspectives due to rate of change. The podcast data provided insight from the company founders, and the 12 departmental leaders employed at the time of the study. Podcasts were published between May 2020 and October 2021. Again, due to rapid growth, replicating this study would require a new podcast series to determine the most current organizational culture artifacts, norms, values, and assumptions.

Lastly, this study incorporated a thorough case study of one company. To provide a broader comparison of creating and sustaining culture, a study of two or more companies would prevent the limitation of singular subject for a study of this kind. Additionally, a study of two startup companies, or a study of a startup company versus a more established, traditional company would be of value for organizational culture research.

Recommendations for Future Research

Based upon findings, future research is encouraged within startup companies, or businesses seeking a culture change. Using Schein's (2004) elements of organizational culture, and significant research on the subject, this study concluded the research remains relevant. This case study reinforced Schein's (2004) framework of artifacts, norms, values, and assumptions with new, innovative means of implementation of the organization's cultures.

This study did not examine the impact of the worldwide pandemic on a business culture. However, considering the impact of business changes due to the pandemic, companies, businesses, departments, and teams could benefit from this organizational culture research as a guide for change management or culture initiatives during this mid to post pandemic time. As business emerge from the pandemic effects, leaders are focusing on employee satisfaction to recruit and retain workers. Future research related to this topic includes leadership and organizational culture and the impact on human capital within companies (Budisusetio et al., 2019).

This topic could be researched further in the context of building teams. This case study subject was a small, startup company. Within a larger organization, this research could expand to incorporate elements of creating and sustaining culture within team units in the business sector and the sports world. An example was Wright's (2019) reference to a story about legendary University of North Carolina basketball coach, Dean Smith. Coach Smith recruited the most talented players for his basketball program. Upon the first meeting between Coach Smith and his players, there was a recurring pattern of players wearing their high school letter jackets. Despite their insight, efforts, goals, and success in high school basketball, Coach Smith required the players to send their high school jacket back home as a visible artifact of their transition to a new system and a new program, college basketball at the University of North Carolina. Similar to a small business, creating and sustaining culture on an athletic team requires significant attention to detail, emotional management of coaches and athletes, and continuous self-assessment.

Driven by the values of the coach, success on the field and court must include development and maintenance of culture (Donoso-Morales et al., 2017).

Further research related to the effects on employees and their impact on the health of an organization would be noteworthy. In today's working world, many companies encourage employees to bring their whole selves to work. It is noteworthy to assess agility and ability to change, emotional intelligence, personality types, and implementation of principles impacting every person within the organization (Greer & Shuck, 2020). Organizations are recruiting and retaining employees by focusing on lifestyle factors. Now more than ever, there is a focus on working conditions, work-life balance, physical and mental health of employees, and impacts of presenteeism related to company successes. A positive organizational culture has impacts on the perceived physical and mental health of employees and employee perceptions of working conditions (Jablonowski, 2017).

To add to this study, research on creating values and associated supporting and non-supporting behaviors could be relevant for teams, business units, or companies of various sizes. Brown's (2018) research was the catalyst for the case study subject company to institute values. From that research and its relationship to this case study research, an expanded exploration of values and organizational culture would be beneficial for the overall topic of organizational culture. Understanding societal beliefs and practices that work their way into organizations and impact culture is of note in creating and updating values during organizational change or growth (Wang & Loundsbury, 2021). Foundational research of organizational culture determined distinct values allow for more autonomy at all levels and prevent top administrators from increasing personal power at the expense of others (Bass & Avolio, 1993). That perspective reinforces Brown's (2018) research on values with an updated, modern approach and an element of interest for future research.

In summary, this study is applicable to a variety of business and professional settings and could be utilized by large companies to small businesses. From research topics associated with employee satisfaction, employee retention, building teams, coaches as organizational culture moderators, and value creation, this study has wide-reaching implications for future organizational culture research. The importance of organizational culture is profound. The findings of this study explain one approach to creating and sustaining organizational culture. Yet, it is one very sound approach that could be utilized as a guide for other companies seeking to create, improve, or sustain their unique organizational culture. So goes the leader, so goes the culture. So goes the culture, so goes the company (Sinek, 2017).

Summary

In conclusion, this chapter presented a discussion of key findings from a case study on the organizational culture of a startup athletic apparel company. Schein's (2004) framework provided the foundation for the case study with data from artifacts, norms and values, and underlying assumptions collected and analyzed from the subject company. The findings determined elements of the framework were present in the structures, processes, and strategies. Implementation of foundational elements by the startup company was new and innovative creating a culture with open communication, defined values, and transparency. The results of the case study indicate the startup athletic apparel company culture is one for a modern business world, and a modern workforce.

To articulate the importance of organizational culture, the leaders of the subject company had a "why". Sinek (2009) determined the premise of leaders identifying "why" started with a positive focus. The creation or improvement of organizational cultures should not focus on starting with what is broken but determine what works and amplify those strengths within the organization. Leaders are responsible to own the narrative from the inside of the organization to the outside with consistency and genuineness. The results of this study indicated the subject company, through values of fun and authenticity, created structures, processes, and strategies to support their "why".

Company founders and leaders created values, an onboarding process, and an openness to grow, listen, and constantly improve for the good of the people within the organization. Each element of the case study provided data to support a culture where people are first. Podcasts, website analysis, and employee surveys provided evidence of authentic care for employees from the CEO and departmental leaders similarly reflected in the perspectives of the employees themselves within the survey data. The efforts of company founders and leaders, driven by research from Brown (2018) related to defining values coupled with their internal systems encouraging feedback and transparency, determined the founders and leaders of the subject company have created and sustained a positive culture within their startup company.

In conclusion, the culture of a company defines its value to those who know it. Culture begins with leaders deciding what they value most. Then, they help everyone in the organization practice behaviors that reflect those values or virtues because what you do is who you are (Horowitz, 2019). Performance metrics can go up and down, but the strength of a culture is the only thing organizations can truly rely on (Sinek, 2017).

Cultures are like precious and prized treasures when they are strong, healthy, and driving the right behaviors. They are among the greatest assets an organization can have (Warrick, 2017).

www.ingramcontent.com/pod-product-compliance
Lightning Source LLC
LaVergne TN
LVHW020436070526
838199LV00063B/4757